S0-AEC-343

DETROIT

BATTLE
OF FALLEN
TIMBERS
FT. MIAMI

FT. DEFIANCE

FT. WAYNE

FT. PITT
(PITTSBURGH)

FT. RECOVERY

PIQUA

CHILLICOTHE

VINCENNES

CAHOKIA

FT. NELSON (LOUISVILLE

KASKASKIA

HARRODSBURG

BOONESBOROUGH

FT. JEFFERSON

N

W

E

S

BK   973.334   D434V   1968
VINCENNES PORTAL TO THE WEST
                                 /DERIETH, A
   1968   .00   FV

3000 204314 30016
St. Louis Community College

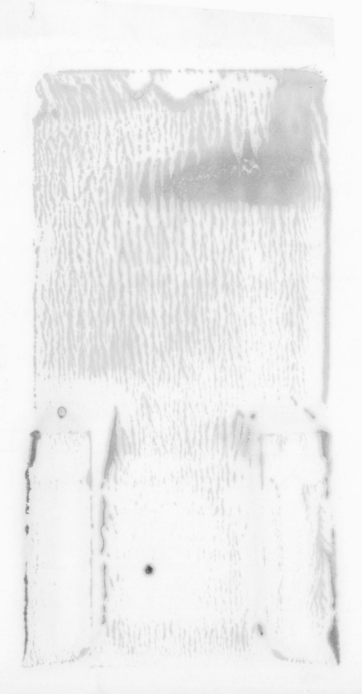

WITHDRAWN

⇢»»»»» VINCENNES: PORTAL TO THE WEST

WITHDRAWN

THE AMERICAN FORTS SERIES

as planned by Stewart H. Holbrook

GUNS AT THE FORKS
(Forts Duquesne and Pitt)
by Walter O'Meara

LOUISBOURG: KEY TO A CONTINENT
by Fairfax Downey

SUTTER'S FORT: GATEWAY TO THE GOLD FIELDS
by Oscar Lewis

THREE FLAGS AT THE STRAITS: THE FORTS OF MACKINAC
by Walter Havighurst

FORT LARAMIE AND THE SIOUX INDIANS
by Remi Nadeau

FORTS OF THE UPPER MISSOURI
by Robert G. Athearn

THUNDERGATE: THE FORTS OF NIAGARA
by Robert West Howard

VINCENNES: PORTAL TO THE WEST
by August Derleth

★ ★ ★

Other Subjects in Preparation

FORT MIMS
by P. D. East

SAGEBRUSH SOLDIERS: THE STORY OF FORT CHURCHILL
by Ferol Egan

FORT LEAVENWORTH
by George Walton

Books by August Derleth

PLACE OF HAWKS *1935*
STILL IS THE SUMMER NIGHT *1937*
WIND OVER WISCONSIN *1938*
RESTLESS IS THE RIVER *1939*
COUNTRY GROWTH *1940*
BRIGHT JOURNEY *1940*
STILL SMALL VOICE: THE BIOGRAPHY OF ZONA GALE *1940*
VILLAGE YEAR: A SAC PRAIRIE JOURNAL *1941*
EVENING IN SPRING *1941*
THE WISCONSIN: RIVER OF A THOUSAND ISLES *1942*
SHADOW OF NIGHT *1943*
THE SHIELD OF THE VALIANT *1945*
VILLAGE DAYBOOK *1947*
THE MILWAUKEE ROAD: ITS FIRST 100 YEARS *1948*
WISCONSIN EARTH *1948*
SAC PRAIRIE PEOPLE *1948*
THE HOUSE OF MOONLIGHT *1953*
PSYCHE *1953*
THE HOUSE ON THE MOUND *1958*
THE MOON TENDERS *1958*
THE HILLS STAND WATCH *1960*
WISCONSIN IN THEIR BONES *1961*
WALDEN WEST *1961*
CONCORD REBEL: A LIFE OF THOREAU *1962*
THE SHADOW IN THE GLASS *1963*
THREE LITERARY MEN *1964*
COUNTRYMAN'S JOURNAL *1964*
WISCONSIN COUNTRY *1965*
COLLECTED POEMS *1967*

VINCENNES:

Portal to the West

<<<<<<<<<<<<<<<<<<<<<<<<<<<<<<<<<<<<<<<<<<<<<<<<<<<<<<<<<<<

By August Derleth

PRENTICE-HALL, INC., Englewood Cliffs, N.J.

2-3-71

Vincennes: Portal to the West
by August Derleth

© 1968 by August Derleth

All rights reserved. No part of this book may be reproduced in any form or by any means, except for the inclusion of brief quotations in a review, without permission in writing from the publisher.

Library of Congress Catalog Card Number: 68-20537

Printed in the United States of America • *T*

PRENTICE-HALL INTERNATIONAL, INC., *London*
PRENTICE-HALL OF AUSTRALIA, PTY. LTD., *Sydney*
PRENTICE-HALL OF CANADA, LTD., *Toronto*
PRENTICE-HALL OF INDIA PRIVATE LTD., *New Delhi*
PRENTICE-HALL OF JAPAN, INC., *Tokyo*

Second printing . . . . . . July, 1969

ACKNOWLEDGMENTS

The sources for this book have been primarily contemporary records left by the participants in the history of the forts at Vincennes, Indiana—particularly George Rogers Clark's own *Campaign in the Illinois;* the letters of Major John Francis Hamtramck collected into *Outpost on the Wabash, 1787–1791,* edited by Gayle Thornbrough, and the *Fort Knox Orderly Book, 1793–1797,* edited by Milo M. Quaife, as well as other letters and documents of the period.

The preparation of this account was furthered appreciably by the cooperation of the staff of the Library of the State Historical Society of Wisconsin and by permission to quote at my discretion from the publications of the Indiana State Historical Society.

My thanks, also, to Paul Vanderbilt and Donald Anderson of the State Historical Society of Wisconsin; Miss Maxine Batman, of the Vincennes Public Library, and J. C. Ohnemus of Vincennes, Indiana.

I am also indebted to the gracious kindness of Mrs. Harry Temple Watts, who gave generously of her time and her authoritative knowledge of history to acquaint me with Vincennes and its background.

PREFACE

It is said—quite truthfully—that the only event of significance that took place at the fort in Vincennes was its capture by George Rogers Clark and his ragged army in 1779. But the importance of that single event can hardly be exaggerated, for it saved the Northwest Territory for the United States, and the forced march Clark and his men made through bitter winter terrain in order to accomplish it is surely one of the great heroic deeds of American history. If it had not been for George Rogers Clark, a very great part of the American heartland might today be under another flag.

It is an ironic circumstance that, after its dramatic part in the American Revolution, the fort at Vincennes played no significant role in the nation's history. Great men passed within sight of its palisades—Tecumseh, the Shawnee leader; William Henry Harrison, the territorial governor in residence at Vincennes; John James Audubon in search of specimens, and others—but the role of the fort, whether it was named "Patrick Henry" or "Knox," was a purely passive one. I could find no record of even a single Indian's having launched an arrow at it, despite such part as its garrison took in pacifying and suppressing the Indians of the territory.

This book, is, accordingly, a straightforward account of the forts at Vincennes, from the founding of the first fort in 1732, to the abandonment of the third Fort Knox in 1816, after the frontier that Clark had helped to carry to the Mississippi had been pushed farther west, one in which the role of the fort—after Clark—was rather a supporting one all too frequently played well behind the front.

—August Derleth

Sauk City, Wisconsin

CONTENTS

I

The Sieur de Vincennes Builds a Fort

About 120 miles above the Arkansas there flows into the Mississippi the Ouabache river formed of four other rivers, one of which rises near Lake Erie and is called the St. Jerome or the Ouabache, the other called the Ohio rises among the Iroquois, and the two others called Tennessee and Cumberland rise near Virginia. The country which these rivers water abounds in wild cattle and is not yet occupied by any European nation.

Since the first of these rivers is the means of communication between Louisiana and Canada, and since this communication will be entirely broken if the English form a settlement at the confluence of one of these three other rivers, which would expose, at the same time, the country of the Illinois and place in danger all the upper country of the colony, the Company has ordered the establishment of a post on the Wabash or Ouabache River...

> —The Company of the Indies to M. Périer, Governor of Louisiana, 30 September 1726. *Sieur de Vincennes Identified,* by Pierre-Georges Roy

1

At the dawn of the eighteenth century, America west of the British colonies along the Atlantic coast and north of the Gulf of Mexico was a vast, unsettled wilderness. His Majesty's Royal Colony of Virginia laid passive claim to a large tract stretching to the shore of the Mississippi; Spain claimed all the Southwest and was eyeing the western shore of the lower Mississippi; and the French were trying—with the support of but without much prac-

tical help from Louis XIV and his ministers—to link French Canada and Louisiana in one great land area. This venture was begun
with the strengthening of the post at Michilimackinac and the
founding of Detroit from the north, while from the south a post
was established at Biloxi and the French began to move up the
Mississippi into the country of the Illinois Indians above the mouth
of the Ohio River, claiming that country as part of Louisiana,
though French settlers from Canada had preceded the French
into Illinois country.

With the Treaty of Utrecht, ending Queen Anne's War in
1713, the French intensified their efforts. Floods, fever, crop fail-
ures, and the threat of the venturesome British from Charleston
had forced the French to retreat from Biloxi to Mobile, and the
French now concentrated on the valley of the Mississippi and its
tributaries. As early as 1702, the then Governor of Louisiana,
Pierre le Moyne, Sieur d'Iberville, persuaded Charles Juchereau
de St. Denys to establish a post at the "mouth of the Wabash,"
then called the "Oubache"—that is to say, at the mouth of the
Ohio, at the site of Cairo, Illinois, for until the middle of the
eighteenth century the Wabash was considered the main stream,
and the Ohio as tributary to it.[1] Juchereau put up a tannery, and
was joined by Fr. Jean Mermet of the Miami mission; he invited
the Mascouten Indians to gather around the post and to hunt for
him, but the venture was short-lived.

The country of the Illinois was of primary interest to the
French. It was the focal point of rivalry and conflict—rivalry
among the French themselves, Canada or New France claiming
jurisdiction to the Ohio from the north, and Louisiana claiming
authority over the Mississippi valley up almost to the Great Lakes
—conflict because of events far from the scene. The westward
movement of the British decades before had strengthened the
Iroquois Confederacy of the Five Nations—the Mohawk, the
Oneida, the Onondaga, the Cayuga, and the Seneca; the Confederacy warred with the Huron and the Algonquin nation of the
St. Lawrence region, and pressed them north and west, upsetting
the balance maintained among the midwestern tribes, particularly
by such wandering Algonquin tribes as the Fox, Sauk, Mascouten,
and Kickapoo, who came into the country north of the Illinois,

then exhausted by war with the Winnebago, allies of the Sioux, which nation occupied the country of the upper Mississippi and land far to the west of that river.

By the time the French began to move north from New Orleans, the Illinois Indians—a tribe of slender and fair-skinned people, vivacious but indolent—were in decline in the country where for so long they had been dominant, having followed the Mound Builders into that country. The main body of the Illinois were to be found in the valley of the Illinois River to the Mississippi. In their decline, the Illinois had separated into lesser tribes—the Kaskaskia, the Peoria, the Cahokia, the Tamaroa, the Moingwena, the Michigamea, and some lesser bands, already fading out at the turn of the century. The near kin of the Illinois were the Miami to the east, in the valley of the Wabash; these included secondary tribes like the Piankeshaw, the Eel River, and the Ouiatenon or Wea Indians. The Miami were constantly at war with tribes south of the Ohio, particularly the Cherokee and the Chickasaw, but tolerated the steady invasion of their country by a sister nation, the Shawnee, moving up from the then Virginia county of Kentucky.

It was into this country between the Wabash River on the east and the Mississippi on the west that the French began to move with the turn of the century. From Canada they came down through the lakes to the headwaters of the Wabash and pushed south. From Louisiana they founded posts at Kaskaskia and Cahokia, and in 1720 erected Fort de Chartres along the Mississippi, 17 miles north of Kaskaskia. From the north, in the same decade, a fort was established at Ouiatenon among the Ouiatenon Indians just below the site of Lafayette, Indiana.

Because the British were threatening to move into the valley of the Wabash by way of the Ohio, representations were made to the Governor of Louisiana urging the establishment of posts and forts to bar the British—particularly one at the junction of the Wabash and the Ohio. British traders, moreover, were already in the area, and the French were handicapped because of the petty jurisdictional squabbling between the governments of Canada and Louisiana. All petitions for a fort at or near the mouth of the Wabash went unheard, for the Company of the Indies, which controlled Louisiana, lacked funds, and for this reason hesitated to add its influence to the pleas for a fort on the Wabash.

In 1724, the Company of the Indies recommended the reduction of the posts among the Illinois and the erection of no new posts. Pierre Dugué, Sieur de Boisbriand, commander at Fort de Chartres, was alarmed at the Company's attitude. He lost no time in pointing out to the Company's officials that if the posts in the Illinois country were reduced, the British would have no trouble winning the Indians away from their tenuous allegiance to the French. The new Governor of Louisiana, Jean Baptiste le Moyne, Sieur de Bienville, added his voice to Boisbriand's, and within a year Boisbriand received instructions to establish a post as near the mouth of the Wabash as was deemed feasible.

But events in that wilderness moved slowly. Governor Bienville could not lay hands on enough merchandise to placate the Indians and assure the French of their loyalty, though the British traders never seemed to suffer any lack of it. Too, Philippe de Rigaud, Marquis de Vaudreuil, Governor of Canada, insisted upon his jurisdiction, though the garrison New France maintained near the present site of Fort Wayne was insufficient to keep out British traders.

Boisbriand, meanwhile, did not wait upon either merchandise or specific orders. He set about recruiting the son of the late commandant at the Ouiatenon post, François (Morganne or Marie) Bissot, Sieur de Vincennes, who, though attached to the French Canadian forces, lent a willing ear to Boisbriand's proposals. Boisbriand had information, however unfounded, that enterprising Dutch traders from Albany had established posts on the upper Ohio, and that British traders had reached the Mississippi, and his urgings spurred the Company of the Indies to greater activity.

On September 30, 1725, the Company of the Indies sent to Périer, the new Governor of Louisiana, a letter proposing that —since Kaskaskia and Cahokia, with Fort de Chartres, held the Mississippi side of the country of the Illinois, and the post among the Ouiatenon the north, an anchor ought to be established in the southeast corner, where the Wabash bent toward the Ohio, thus securing the area—either along the Wabash itself or at the mouth of the Tennessee River.

"M. Périer will reflect well on this subject," the official wrote, "and consider if, by giving eight or ten soldiers to the said Sieur de Vincennes, with the missionary destined for the Ouabache, he will not find himself in condition to assure, by the Indians, the communication between Louisiana and Canada, and to prevent the English from penetrating into our colony, without obliging the Company to construct a fort on the lower Ouabache, of which the expense of the establishment and the support of the garrison make an object of consequence."

To facilitate this venture, Vincennes was confirmed as a half-pay lieutenant attached to Louisiana, though he was not formally detached from Canada. He was then a young man just as old as the century—26. It was hoped that he could persuade a large body of Indians to settle at the place he chose to establish a post wherever he thought best at the bend of the Wabash, since the King and his ministers seemed to be reluctant to send into the American provinces any substantial number of colonists. The King, however, did instruct the Governor of Canada to release Vincennes for the purpose of establishing the fort on the Wabash.

Delays, notwithstanding orders and instructions, were integral to life in the wilderness. It took a year before Governor Périer got around to sending a load of goods to supply the still non-existent post on the Wabash, but the boat set out from New Orleans so late that it encountered ice and had to turn back. And the next spring Vincennes fell ill, and remained in poor health until midsummer. In the meantime, the Company of the Indies stipulated that the new post was to be manned by ten soldiers and two officers. The Company fixed upon three hundred livres as sufficient for the construction of the fort, and 1,170 livres as pay for the men during the initial year of their occupation of the post. As for presents for the Indians, the Company estimated that 800 livres ought to be enough.

Périer immediately objected to the niggardliness of the allowance. But such parsimony was all too typical of the official approach to the problem of establishing posts and maintaining good relations with the Indians. Périer made clear that the Company was allowing only half enough money to build the fort, and scarcely a fourth of the sum that would be needed if the French were to compete on anything like an equal basis with the British for the favor of the Indians.

When he recovered, Vincennes was in no hurry to select a site for the post on the Wabash. He went back to live for a while with the Miami at Ouiatenon, but there is some reason to believe that he had already made a tentative selection of the Wabash site, though the building of the fort waited upon a more favorable occasion. At some time during 1727 Vincennes and a small group of soldiers made their way down the Wabash and fixed upon a site for the new post—not at the mouth of that river, after all, but approximately a hundred and fifty miles up river from the junction of the Wabash and the Ohio. The post was first called Poste des Pianguichats, after Indians found in the vicinity [2]—one of the numerous branches of the Miami, who had made themselves at home among the remains of the settlement left by the first inhabitants of the area, the Mound Builders, long since vanished.

The site chosen for the post lay along the Wabash in relatively low, flat terrain, with some knolls and low hills bounding it. Vincennes obviously had an eye for settlement, not alone for the building of an isolated fort, for which he might have found a less pregnable position. The chosen site appeared to him to be a fertile one, a site to which French settlers could be drawn; it was a country of many trees—beech, pawpaw, persimmon, sycamore, maple, linden, pecan, red gum, tulip, aspen, ash, cottonwood, elm, wild plum, oak, black locust, and some juniper—one that afforded its wild life, which included elk, raccoons, opossums, wolves, foxes, and porcupines, all manner of natural food—nuts, persimmons, wild strawberries, mulberries, wild apples, and other food commonly found in the wilderness of the continent's heartland. It was a country which, already supporting much game as well as a great variety of fish in its streams—sturgeon, catfish, pike, perch, bass, suckers, mullets and pickerel being the most common —would certainly fit well into the plans of the French governors for the strengthening of French control by enduring settlement.

Despite the characteristic lack of vigor with which the King and his ministers pressed colonization of the region, Vincennes, when he returned from his stay among the Miami, persisted. Limitations notwithstanding, he had built a fort by early 1732, and on March 7 of that year he wrote to one of the officials of the Marine in France a letter typical of many that he was to write:

> I begin by informing you that the Wabash is composed of five nations who compose four villages of which the least has sixty men carrying arms, and all of them could furnish from six to seven hundred men if it were necessary to assemble them for the welfare of the service and for their own welfare. On account of the nearness of the English, it has been impossible for me to bring together all these nations because there has always been a lack of merchandise in this place. The fort which I have built is about eighty miles in the Wabash country up the river by which the English have been able to descend and open up commerce with these nations. The place is very suitable in which to build a great settlement which I would have done if I had had troops enough. In regard to the commerce which one can carry on here, a traffic in skins could go on all year to the extent of 30,000 skins.

The Indians, however, wooed by both the French and the English, were troublesome:

> I have never had a greater need of troops in these places than at the present time. The savages, the Illinois, as well as the Miami and others are more insolent than they have ever been, especially since the Foxes were defeated. The little experience which I have acquired in the twenty years that I have been among them, causes me to fear some evil trick on the part of these nations and above all, of my own who, seeing a settlement which I had begun, did not seem to wish it to be continued. Since for three years nothing has happened. Except, Monsieur, the migration of all the nations not only of the lakes but also of other places.

Vincennes had no illusions about the "friendship" of the Indians, knowing that that friendship had its price, which the British were far more successful in meeting than were the French, who were forever deprived of merchandise for trade and gifts by the short-sighted insularity of the officials to whom Vincennes and other French commanders addressed repeated representations.

You do me the honor to indicate to me that I send you a statement of the work done and to be done. There is only one fort and
two houses within and it will be necessary very soon to build a
guard house with barracks in which to lodge the soldiers. Nothing
else is possible in this place with so few troops. I need thirty men
with an officer. I am more embarrassed than ever, in this place,
by the war with the Chickasaws, who have come twice since
spring. Only two days ago the last party took away three people
and since the French took up tomahawks against them I am
obliged every day to put up a defense. I hope, that of your good-
ness, you will indeed wish to give your attention to this place
and to my difficulty for myself as well as for the little garrison
which I have. This is the favor which he awaits, from you, who
has the honor to be, with profound respect, M., your very humble
and very obedient servant, Vincennes.[3]

Vincennes's superiors did little to alleviate his needs. Five years
earlier, when he had selected the site for the fort beside the
Wabash where it bent southwestward, the Governor and the superior of the Jesuits in Louisiana had enthusiastically followed up
his report by dispatching one Father d'Outreleau to "the mission
of the Wabash." The Jesuit never reached the site. He had started
on his journey too late in the season, and he found the river in-
hospitable; indeed, he lost all the supplies and materials for the
building of a house and church and was fortunate to have saved
his life. In the ensuing debate about who was to replace the
lost chapel and indemnify the Jesuit order, "the mission of the
Wabash" was forgotten, and Father d'Outreleau was sent elsewhere.

Within a month of his earlier letter, Vincennes had to write
again to say that the post lacked everything, to complain that he
was obliged to borrow from travelers and to use his own funds
to meet daily expenses. Vincennes was not absolutely isolated,
for his post had been established near the Buffalo Trace, and
occasional travelers came by. But he did have to ask for reim-
bursement. Furthermore, without merchandise, he had a difficult
time appeasing even the friendliest of the Piankeshaw, the local
Indians, and he could not hope to make any progress with Indians friendly to the British because he could not compete.

All the enterprise of Vincennes and other men like him in the wilderness domain of the French was lost in the deliberations and delays of their superiors. French colonial policy in relation to the American provinces was apparently steeped in irresolution complicated by ignorance and unwillingness to accept the advice of the governors on the scene.

When, later in the spring of 1732, Vincennes persuaded another village of Piankeshaw to move to the new settlement from one sixty miles up river, he was hard put to it to make it worth their while. Of encouragement in words he received much, of coin of the realm or merchandise virtually none.

Nevertheless, Vincennes did everything in his power to establish a settlement as well as a fort at the site. In 1733, having built a house apart from the fort, he married the daughter of Philippe Longpré of Kaskaskia, and lost no time in fathering two daughters, Marie Therese and Catherine. Despite the shortage of goods, he kept the local Indians friendly. But, though the land was fertile, and the Indians—when they were impelled to do so, raised maize, beans, squash, and other vegetables, and found the country replete with wild game as the river was with fish—colonists could not readily be lured to a site so deep in the wilderness.

Vincennes's labors were still further complicated by the return to the governorship of Louisiana of Bienville, who came filled with plans to destroy the power of all the Indians in the Illinois territory who remained friendly to the British—particularly the Chickasaw. He began by ordering Robert Groston, Sieur de St. Ange, commander at Fort de Chartres, to prepare the Indians of northern Illinois to fight the tribes whose allegiance was commanded by the British. He undoubtedly sent orders of a similar nature to Vincennes, for both commanders replied in protest—St. Ange to say that the Indians within range of his command were sufficiently ill humored without adding a further cause of irritation and Vincennes to say frankly that the Indians within reach of the post on the Wabash were dissatisfied with the meager supplies the French had given them. Vincennes added pointedly that many of them were once again actively trading with the English, who were in consequence getting the best of their furs.

Once again Vincennes pointed out that his garrison was too

small to exercise any real control over the Indians. Once again he asked for a force of at least thirty men and an officer. In addition, the fort, which was stoutly built of wood, was in need of a stone veneer if it was intended to withstand attack. It also had to be enlarged if reinforcements were to be sent, for it contained at the moment of writing barracks only for the small detachment there, plus a house for himself, which he had built at his own expense.

As a result of this frustration of his plans, Bienville was moved to action. He relieved St. Ange of his command at Fort de Chartres and put in his place Captain d'Artaguiette, who was far younger and more active. He was satisfied with Vincennes and wrote of him to Paris that he was very useful to the colony: "He is a Canadian, son of an officer of the infantry in Canada, is brave, active, knows the government of the Miamis among whom he has been for fifteen years." He meant to strengthen the fort and the position at Vincennes, but before he could do so the smoldering grievances of the Chickasaw broke out in war between them and the French early in 1733. The Chickasaw had been allied to the British for some time, and the failure of the French to supply them with merchandise only confirmed their allegiance to the British. The additional men intended for Vincennes were forgotten.

Despite the relative exposure of Vincennes to attack, the war —such as it was—stayed to the north. Governor Beauharnois of Canada continued to urge the Indians of the north to attack the Chickasaw, and some Indians did move south—having received a pipe and belt from Beauharnois—with the intention of doing battle, but none ever engaged the Chickasaw, in part, certainly, because the two French governors could not agree on the best time to strike. Beauharnois argued for spring, but Bienville held out for autumn, when, as he pointed out, the French and their allies could live on the provisions the Chickasaw had stored for the winter season—assuming that the invaders could capture them.

With the failure of a general Indian war to materialize, the Sieur de Vincennes applied to the governor of Canada for permission to journey north to take care of some family matters; he neglected to ask for leave from Bienville, though he did write to say that he was starting north only because there appeared to be no danger to Vincennes among the Indians in the vicinity.

He returned to his post the following winter, complaining bitterly that, though he had persuaded "a hundred" Canadian families to migrate to the site of the fort on the Wabash, Governor Beauharnois would not grant them permission to leave Canada. On Vincennes's return Bienville at last ordered the thirty desired men to go to the Wabash post; they were to be supplied by d'Artaguiette from Fort de Chartres. He wrote to d'Artaguiette that he considered the Wabash post one of the most important in the Louisiana colony. And so it was, if the line against the British was to be held.

For the British were moving relentlessly down the Ohio. Their trade in the valley of that river steadily increased. The post on the Wabash was in their path, though they had long since crossed the Wabash to the north and traders were active among the Piankeshaw and Miami nations.

Vincennes hoped to make inroads in the British trade. To start, he expected to persuade a village of Piankeshaw along the Wabash to the north—most of whose inhabitants had been trading with the British—to move down to his post, at one and the same time securing his position and cutting the Indians off from the British while the French took over their trade.

Unhappily, the French officials were no more responsive to Vincennes's pleas for trading goods than they had ever been. America was remote from Paris, and the problems of the French commanders viewed from that distance seemed minimal, even unreal. Vincennes wrote for "shirts, guns, mirrors, combs, hats, powder, 'English' cloth, shoes, collars, and 2943 pounds of flour" —all of which were missing from a previous order he had sent.[4] This seems to have been the prevailing tenor of Vincennes's letters to Bienville.

The Indians, in turn, complained bitterly that the French could not be depended upon. Discontent spread even to the French soldiers, who were in any case, immured as they were in the wilderness, prone to discontent. By the spring of 1735, five soldiers had deserted the Wabash post to join the British. Such desertions were common in neighboring posts, particularly Fort de Chartres. The British had more trading goods to offer the Indians and more merchandise with which to reward turncoats; they unceasingly pressed their advantage, hoping to drive a wedge between the two French provinces in America. At the same time, the British encouraged the militant Chickasaw to foment trouble.

By late 1735, Governor de Bienville, exasperated by reports from the outposts of the colony, concluded that the only solution lay in war with the Chickasaw. He needed a pretext for making war and did not have far to look for one. In the course of a recent war with the Natchez Indians, some of the Natchez had escaped from French soldiers and taken refuge with the Chickasaw south of the Ohio; Bienville now demanded that the Chickasaw surrender the fugitives. The Chickasaw, who had been interfering for a long time with the movements of French traders, soldiers and settlers and who, like the Chickasaw north of the Ohio, were trading with the British, refused to give up the Natchez, as the Governor of Louisiana had foreseen. When his ultimatum was rejected, Bienville had the pretext he wanted.

He had his plans made. He, with an army composed of French soldiers and their Choctaw Indian allies, would march north. Artaguiette, with a smaller force of soldiers, *habitants* and Indians from the Illinois country, and Vincennes, with his Miami Indians and some Iroquois, would march to join the Governor at a rendezvous fixed for Écors à Prud'homme, a post on the east bank of the Mississippi not far from the present town of Fulton, Tennessee. The date fixed for the meeting was March 10, 1736. Once the three forces had joined, a considerable army would be ranged against the Chickasaw.

The major part of that army, however, was under Bienville's direction, and, in the manner typical of French officials, Bienville did not start on time. He did not leave Mobile until April 1, and as a result both Artaguiette and Vincennes reached the rendezvous some days before the fixed date. The two companies promptly erected a fort of stones and sent scouts to look for Bienville.

The scouts had hardly returned, with no word of Bienville's whereabouts, when runners came into camp from the north with the announcement that he had sent word up the Mississippi to the Illinois forts that he and his army could not reach the rendez-vous until the end of April or the beginning of May. Artaguiette conveyed this information to the French allies in a council of war at once. The Indians were dismayed. In order to travel swiftly and light, they had brought along only enough provisions to see them into battle—not enough to keep them for a month of idling while Bienville found time to move north. Their remaining in camp was not a matter of choice; they lacked the provisions to do so and had to return.

They pointed out, however, that scouts had discovered a Chickasaw village not too far from the camp and removed from the greatest concentration of Chickasaw. An assault could be made on this village, and enough provisions could be captured to make possible their staying with the French. Artaguiette and Vincennes had no alternative but to agree, particularly as the search for Bienville had already taken precious time and the month of March was waning.

On the night of March 24, the war party moved into position near the village, French and Indian allies deploying themselves in the most advantageous manner. They waited out the night and attacked at dawn. Unfortunately, it was unlikely that so large a party of French soldiers and Indians could have gone unnoticed in enemy territory. The Chickasaw were well aware of their presence—not only those in the village under attack but also those in the central encampment of Chickasaw. Furthermore, the move-ment of the soldiers toward the village could scarcely have been unobserved.

The battle had only begun, when several hundred Chickasaw poured in from the woods around the village. Their appearance so dismayed and frightened some of the attacking forces that the Miami fled at once. The French, the Iroquois and the Arkansas Indians were left alone. The battle raged intensely for a while, but the Chickasaw were much superior in numbers, and the French, with their allies, suffered a disastrous defeat.

Artaguiette died in action. Those members of his attacking party who were not slain or could not manage to escape were taken prisoner. One of them, Rickarville, who made his escape

months later with the help of British traders among the Chickasaw, said that the prisoners were taken into the Chickasaw village
and burned at the stake in an orgy that lasted from three in the
afternoon until midnight.

Among the prisoners who were put to the stake was François
Bissot, Sieur de Vincennes, who had established the fort and the
settlement along the lower Wabash and given the latter his name.

2

Bienville, meanwhile, started north for the rendezvous that
he had not kept on time. Evidently no word of the defeat and
death of Artaguiette and Vincennes reached him, which suggests
that all the responsible officers of the defeated party had been
killed. Spring was well advanced, and the going could not have
been easy, what with flood waters in many places; the expedition
made slow progress. Instead of reaching the rendezvous within
a month, the forces took closer to two, so that it was late in May
when Bienville and his war party reached Écors à Prud'homme.

The Governor was astonished to find no one at the rendezvous.
He angrily blamed Artaguiette for failing him and sent out scouts,
thinking that Artaguiette and Vincennes and their allies could not
be far away. He was even more outraged and dismayed to learn
from his scouts that the only white men to be seen in the entire
area were British traders.

Between him and Fort de Chartres lay hostile country, and the
presence of British traders only underscored the danger of traveling through it without a considerably larger force. Reluctantly,
Bienville ordered a retreat, and the ill-conceived campaign came
to an ignominious end.

Reports of the disaster inflicted upon Artaguiette and Vincennes, sent down from Fort de Chartres, awaited Bienville in
New Orleans. There were letters from various officers, among
them the old commander among the Illinois, St. Ange, who
recommended that his son, Louis de Bellerive de St. Ange, be
appointed to command the post at Vincennes.

Bienville paid heed to the elder St. Ange's solicitation and
wrote to his superiors on the young man's behalf, "At present, he

is commanding a small post on the Missouri, and a long time ago M. d'Artaguitte spoke to me of him, as being a brave boy and of great merit." The French officials, however, moved no faster in an emergency than otherwise. Bienville followed this letter of June with another recommendation in October.

Young St. Ange was an appreciably more dedicated man than was Vincennes. Furthermore, he well understood his task, which was not an easy one and which was made the more difficult because the post on the Wabash had been essentially one man's post. Though St. Ange had had previous occasions to make peace among the Indians, particularly the Piankeshaw and the Illinois, he had then been among the Illinois, and the Piankeshaw at Vincennes therefore distrusted him. Many of Vincennes's Piankeshaw deserted the post to join kinsmen up the Wabash at Vermilion. At St. Ange's arrival late in 1736, the fort was not adequately protected, and its use as a trading post was accordingly diminished.

Furthermore, British traders had persuaded Cherokee and Chickasaw to establish villages on the Ohio. Bienville impulsively concluded, in the face of this intelligence, that the fort on the lower Wabash was hardly worth maintaining and decided that it ought to be moved all the way down to the mouth of the Ohio. He did actually send orders to St. Ange for the removal of the fort, but, perhaps because of some disagreement among the French officials, the orders were never carried out.

But the removal the following year of the Cherokee and the Chickasaw from the Ohio—where they clearly threatened the fort on the lower Wabash—very probably diminished the force of Bienville's argument for the establishment of a new fort at the mouth of the Wabash. It is likely though that the refusal of the Wabash Indians to settle the new site, their reason being that the place chosen for the fort and the surrounding region were inundated in periods of high water on the Wabash and the Ohio, added some weight to the opposition to the abandonment of Vincennes's post.

St. Ange went ahead with badly needed repairs to the fort left by Vincennes. It needed to be strengthened, and it needed stone facing. He took steps toward replacing the Indians who had left the area for the north, and at his urging a small band

of Indians settled not far away at the site of Russellville, Illinois.
But it was clear to St. Ange that what the post at Vincennes
needed primarily was not Indians but French settlers, and this
problem he could not resolve without help from the government,
for the settlers were reluctant to come unless they could own
the land they settled.

Bienville, however, still nursed his plan to remove the post to
the mouth of the Ohio and was of little help. Yet, in 1742, the
Piankeshaw remaining at Vincennes—no doubt with the consent
of the Miami nation of which they were part—surrendered the
territory trapped by the French to the French. It was a larger
territory than that occupied by Vincennes, one embracing more
than a million and a half acres lying north and east of Vincennes,
though Congress later reduced the amount for Vincennes to five
thousand acres, which were given to the Borough of Vincennes
and later became known as the "Vincennes Common."

Settlement at Vincennes became more attractive. The government at New Orleans did little to cooperate with St. Ange. Bienville was replaced in 1743 by Governor Vaudreuil, who promised
to make the French fur trade once more a flourishing business.
He expected to send more traders among the Indians in the
colony and intended by this means to increase the influence of
the French, thus weakening that of the British. In the face of
the niggardliness with which the French government served the
colonies' needs, however, this goal was sheer naïveté.

Together with this dream—indeed, to his mind an important
part of it—was Vaudreuil's decision to establish a new fort at or
near the mouth of the Ohio, one of stone and meant to be a key
fort. Whether it would be Bienville's fort at the mouth of the
Wabash or at the mouth of the Ohio was not immediately clear.
The important aspect was that its presence would check the expansion of the British, who were well on the way to cutting all
communications between the two French provinces. He expected
to bring to the new fort the Kickapoo and Mascouten (who, he
believed, were willing to abandon their village at *Terre Haute*),
as well as the Shawnee, some of whom had come down the Ohio
and seemed agreeable.

Implementation of Vaudreuil's plans clearly implied the abandonment of the Vincennes post. St. Ange himself had at one time had some doubt about the post's utility. Not long after taking it over, he had briefly despaired of improving it to the extent necessary in the face of the desertion of the Piankeshaw. In 1737 the general impression given to the Company of the Indies was summarized in a letter by M. Salmon, who wrote of a representative: "He adds that he has never seen to the present time that this post was of much utility, and that it causes much expense. For myself, I think that really it is more expensive than useful." But he added cautiously, "However, it will be important to maintain it to keep the English from establishing there, which they will certainly do if we abandon it." [5]

By 1743, however, when Vaudreuil came to the governorship, St. Ange had established himself. Indeed, the post was for a while called "St. Ange" or "St. Anne," though to Bienville it remained the fort of the Piankeshaw and to the traders it was more commonly known as the "little Weas" or "Little Wiaut," both names meaning "Little Ouiatenon" after the Ouiatenon Indians, to which the Piankeshaw were believed to belong. But the name "Vincennes" was even more widely and persistently applied to the post and to the settlement, such as it was.

The settlement was slow to grow. The Piankeshaw village had been called "Chip-pe-co-ke," which meant "scrub brush," but it was now largely deserted. Though the surrender of the Indian lands in 1742 was intended to stimulate settlement by the French, the post at Vincennes was referred to as late as 1746 as "quite inconsiderable," having "about 40 men and 5 negroes," whose occupation was "hunting and the culture of wheat and tobacco." [6] St. Ange was anxious for the settlement to grow, for he wanted to counter Vaudreuil's plan for a fort at the mouth of the Ohio, where, he had been informed, the soil was rich, buffalo were plentiful and the French could deliver goods by water far more inexpensively than the British could carry them over the mountains.

Settlement was expedited by gifts of the commandant at the post, particularly of titles to land. Very probably Vincennes issued no land grants, as the land was in his time still claimed by the Indians. But St. Ange did so, though because of lack of registration no record has been left. The earliest record of a deed is of

one issued to François Racine dit Beauchêne, though this deed
was lost and was validated by the Federal government long after
it was given. The first deed on the legal records of Vincennes
was issued in April 1750 to François Filiatreau. None seems to
have been for any very great land area; most of the French interested in settling wanted grants of areas about 150 feet square
—enough space for a house, perhaps a summer kitchen, an out-
house, a storage building for pork, a place to keep chickens, a
stable, perhaps a garden plot and an orchard. And, because the
early settlers were engaged in trading, they preferred their land
to be located on or near the fort, whereas those French settlers
who hoped to engage in farming preferred their land to run back
from the shore of the Wabash and liked to own areas of "two
by forty arpents," which came to somewhat more than 68 acres.[7]

While St. Ange was doing all in his limited power to make
Vincennes more valuable to the Province of Louisiana and the
Governor of that province was holding to his decision to establish
a central fort at the mouth of the Ohio, the British were pushing
steadily westward from the Atlantic seaboard. Furthermore, they
continued to have a marked advantage over the French traders,
offering more merchandise for trade and more generous terms.
And because they took their furs from more northern latitudes,
the furs were of generally better quality than the French managed
to collect to the south of the zone invaded by British traders. The
posts in the Illinois country and the region of the lower Wabash
and Ohio customarily took in inferior furs.

The British were also, despite edicts from England, considerably less hampered in their expansion. Though Charles I of
England had imposed proscriptions early in the century, the British colonies were so widespread and already so well populated
that it was impossible to enforce them. But when, in 1742, the
French King, aping the colonial policy of the British, forbade all
manufacture of salable goods in New France and ordered that
all pelts, gems and minerals gathered in New France be shipped
to the industries of France in exchange for manufactures, it was
relatively easy to enforce the law because the French were of
necessity living in small communities under military comman-
dants. They were thus required to work much harder than the

British, and they were also more vigilant against the depredations of the Indians, though these raids abated in direct proportion to the increase in settlement. Nor did the French settlers find it easy to deal with their superiors and their government; those hardy Frenchmen who did come up the Mississippi or down through the lakes to settle the Illinois country from the Mississippi to the Wabash and the Ohio had to deal with New Orleans and Quebec, which were not only far away but were also in themselves without sufficient authority to settle the problems of the settlers and the posts.

During much of the decade that followed St. Ange's assumption of command at Vincennes, England and France were at war because of France's part in the War of the Austrian Succession. Though the war was not prosecuted with any vigor in America— the British seized Fort Louisbourg on Cape Breton Island, and the French and their Indian allies assaulted Albany and burned Saratoga in 1745—it did offer greater incentives for British penetration of the Illinois country. The inconclusive Treaty of Aix-la-Chapelle in 1748, beyond restoring Fort Louisbourg to the French and in general affirming the prewar status quo, had little effect on the Illinois country.

Nevertheless, the British colonies were determined to push to the west from Pennsylvania and Virginia. Such Ohio Valley traders as George Croghan and Conrad Weiser greatly expanded their posts and, acting for the Pennsylvania legislature, made allies of the Indians in the vicinity. Christopher Gist was sent out to explore the upper Ohio for the Ohio Company, and a trading post rose at Cumberland. By 1749, the date of the "lost" title at Vincennes, the French government had sent out Céleron de Bienville to take control of the Ohio Valley by force. In the course of this campaign, Charles Langlade led forces to attack the British trading post at Pickawillany. Pierre-Paul de la Malgue, Sieur de Marin, established Fort Presque Isle near the present site of Erie and Fort le Boeuf at the portage to French Creek, and seized Venango from the British traders where French Creek joins the Alleghany, renaming it Fort Machault.

In 1754 the young George Washington, dispatched to protest the action of the French and to inquire into their intentions, returned to report that they clearly meant to take and hold the entire Ohio Valley and that, in his opinion, they could not be dislodged by any means short of force. In that same year, hostilities began.

It was not immediately apparent—certainly not to the residents of Vincennes—that it was the beginning of a major struggle. It was begun by the British, who, hoping to forestall the French, decided to build a fort at the Forks of the Ohio—the junction of the Allegheny and Monongahela Rivers. This decision was taken in late winter of 1754, but before the following spring had run its course the French had seized the site and built Fort Duquesne there. George Washington headed a force of soldiers sent to seize Fort Duquesne. He won a skirmish with a French reconnaissance party, then built a fort named "Necessity" at Great Meadows. There he was attacked by the French under Coulon de Villiers and was forced to capitulate.

All this conflict had little effect on Vincennes, save that a few volunteers from that post went to take part in the defense of Fort Duquesne. After the cession of land by the Indians twelve years before, Vincennes had begun slowly to grow. French-Canadians came to settle there, taking up land on three sides of the fort and back from the Wabash.

With the country around the fort relatively calm and quiet, St. Ange turned his attention to the development of the settlement. The fort itself was improved and repaired. St. Ange undertook to build a chapel next to the fort; he named it "St. Francis Xavier" in honor of the Jesuit priest, Father Francis Xavier de Guinne, who visited the settlement from time to time. He laid out and opened two streets—Busseron Street and Rue de St. Honoré, which led away from the front gates of the fort.

There remained the constant danger of Indian attack, particularly as information reached the fort that the British were patching up all their quarrels with the Indians, including the wavering Iroquois, with whom Benjamin Franklin and other delegates from New England, Pennsylvania, Maryland and New York had conferred at the behest of the British government. They had drawn up a plan of union—a patent indication that the British meant to use their Indian allies against the French. But nothing in the way of unusual depredations by the Indians against the French took place. The settlement was accustomed to learning that an occasional traveler had been set upon and robbed—perhaps killed—by marauding Indians, and British traders were beginning to appear within range of the fort's command, but no event of an untoward nature took place.

The government in Louisiana changed its head. Vaudreuil was replaced by Kerlerec, who adopted his predecessor's hope for a post at the mouth of the Ohio. He understood also that it was necessary to supply more goods to the Indians if the French expected to keep their trade. South of the Ohio the British had busily established posts among the Cherokee, whereas to the north the French had done nothing. Kerlerec seemed to have convinced himself that increased trade with the resident and other friendly Indians along the Wabash and the Ohio, together with establishment of a post at the mouth of the Ohio and the removal of the post at Vincennes, would improve the French position to the point at which the British would be rash to challenge it. Once a fort had been built at the mouth of the Ohio, he wrote, "The one of St. Ange [Vincennes] will then become useless, but it can be moved 40 or 50 leagues above on the Ohio River and re-established firmly." [8]

None of Governor Kerlerec's plans came to maturity, for events moved too swiftly. His plans had hardly been formulated when the French were locked in mortal struggle with the British and their Indian allies—a struggle that came to be known as the "French and Indian War." It had begun at the Forks of the Ohio scarcely a year after Kerlerec had replaced Vaudreuil and was now being pressed since the arrival of General Edward Braddock in Virginia in mid-April 1755. The early defeat and death of Braddock by the French and their Indian allies at the battle of the Monongahela below Fort Duquesne did not materially lessen the pressure of the British; on the contrary, forces of New Englanders and regulars under Colonels Robert Monckton and John Winslow captured the French Fort Beauséjour in mid-June, and by the end of that month the Bay of Fundy was under British control.

Vaudreuil's—and Kerlerec's—dream of forts at the Cumberland, the Tennessee and the mouth of the Ohio faded and died. The expulsion of the Acadians from Nova Scotia had sent a tremor through all New France, and, though the British thereafter suffered setbacks at the hand of Louis Joseph, Marquis de Montcalm —who had come to Canada from France following the loss of Nova Scotia and had taken and destroyed Forts Oswego, George and William Henry—it was evident to French officials in New France that Great Britain under William Pitt was committed to continuing warfare.

By the end of 1759 it was evident that the French position throughout New France had so seriously eroded that repair was virtually impossible. Fort Niagara was taken, Fort Carillon was blown up, Quebec surrendered and within another year all Canada, under its governor Pierre de Rigaud, Marquis de Vaudreuil, had surrendered. To the north of Vincennes, Detroit was in the hands of Major Robert Rogers, and all the Great Lakes posts once controlled by the French had fallen to the British.

On February 10, 1763, the Treaty of Paris ended the French and Indian War. By its terms France ceded to Great Britain all its claims to Canada and the territory east of the Mississippi except for the city of New Orleans. Throughout the years of hostilities—and though the British had seized a French fort as close as that at Ouiatenon above Vincennes—the post commanded by St. Ange took part in no engagement.

Nor were the British in any haste to take over Vincennes. They were principally engaged from May through November of 1763 in dealing with the destructively successful uprising of Indians led by the Ottawa chief, Pontiac, who scourged the region from Niagara west to Detroit, which withstood a seige of five months until Pontiac lifted it in November. Under Pontiac, the Indians had destroyed Fort Sandusky, Fort St. Joseph, Fort Miami, Fort Ouiatenon, Fort Venango, Fort Le Boeuf, Fort Presque—the fort at Vincennes escaped.

Not until the rebellion led by Pontiac had been crushed did the British think again of Vincennes. In May 1764 St. Ange was ordered to take command at Fort de Chartres and to hold it until the British called upon him to turn it over to them. On May 18 he delivered a farewell address to the garrison and people of Vincennes, and, turning the post over to Major Joseph Antoine Drouët, Sieur de Richardville, who was assisted by François de Coindre, he departed for Chartres, leaving behind him close to seventy families, most of them French-Canadians.

II

George Rogers Clark

❦

The Wabash is a beautiful River, with high and upright banks, less subject to overflow, than any other River (the Ohio excepted) in this part of America. It discharges itself into the Ohio, one thousand and twenty-two miles below Fort Pitt.... The land on this River is remarkably fertile, and several parts of it are natural meadows, of great extent, covered with fine long grass. The timber is large, and high, and in such variety, that almost all the different kinds growing upon the Ohio, and its branches, may be found here.... Two French settlements are established on the Wabash, called Post Vincent and Ouiatanon; the first is 150 miles, and the other 262 miles from its mouth. The former is on the eastern side of the River, and consists of 60 settlers and their families. They raise Indian corn,—Wheat; and Tobacco of an extraordinary good quality.... They have a fine breed of horses (brought originally by the Indians from the Spanish settlements on the western side of the River Mississippi) and large stocks of Swine, and Black Cattle. The settlers deal with the natives for Furrs and Deer skins, to the amount of 5000 l. annually. Hemp of a good texture grows spontaneously in the low lands of the Wabash, as do Grapes in the greatest abundance, having a black, thin skin, of which the inhabitants in the Autumn, make a sufficient quantity (for their own consumption) of well-tasted Red-Wine....

> —Thomas Hutchins, *A Topographical Description of Virginia, Pennsylvania, Maryland, and North Carolina.* 1778

1

The British virtually ignored the fort at Vincennes.

Once they were in control in all the country east of the Mississippi, from the Great Lakes to the Gulf of Mexico, the British looked upon Vincennes as of no significance. Apart from the Sieur de Richardville, who had been named by St. Ange to command the post, the British permitted the settlers at Vincennes to select their own leaders. When Richardville died on April 15, 1765, they named Nicolas Chappart—chosen by the settlers—to succeed him. And when Chappart in turn died in 1770, they named, again at the behest of the population, Jean Baptiste Racine dit Ste. Marie. Though St. Ange was relieved of his command of Fort de Chartres by Captain Thomas Sterling on October 10, 1765, French commanders continued in control of Vincennes.

Vincennes, however, was visited freely by the British in unofficial capacities. The former French territory was under martial law, and the French had until August 10, 1764, to leave the territory. Well before that time, however, the British had concluded —having taken the time and opportunity to travel through as much of the former French territory as possible—that they could not administer the area without the help of the old French settlers. Furthermore, the strictures of Sir William Johnson, the Superintendent of Indian Affairs for the British—strictures that included the evacuation of the French from the fur fields—proved impractical. Martial law was lifted in September 1764, and the "commanders" at Vincennes became civil officers, that is, mayors, with the power to grant land patents and generally to conduct the affairs of the settlement.

In 1766 Captain Frazer, writing to General Haldimand, the British governor, said that there were "sixty families living" in Vincennes, "who raised a considerable quantity of wheat, tobacco, and have a good stock of cattle." When Lieutenant John Rumsey arrived to take command of the old fort for the British in 1766, he found it sadly deteriorated. Nevertheless, he repaired it and renamed it "Fort Sackville," then made a census for his superiors.

Rumsey listed no fewer than 232 men, women and children

and 168 "strangers"—who may have been a floating population of hunters, travelers and traders coming in from the east. He also enumerated 352 oxen, 558 cows, 260 horses, 295 hogs, 3 mills, 18 tons of tobacco and 10,870 bushels of corn.[1] Colonel Wilkens, evidently on a mission for the British General Gage, reported subsequently that "at Post Vincent, there is no other Money passes but Peltry and generally Furrs, but I can assure Your Excellency that no other person Except Bayntin & Company [2] have given Bond that their Peltry shall be landed at a British Market. And it is certain that their is not one Twentieth part of the Trade in this Country, all the rest must of Consequence go to the French Markets." [3]

The continuing reports of trouble-making "strangers," many maliciously inspired by self-seeking traders, coupled with reports of frequent French violations of the rules regarding trade, alarmed General Gage, who was stirred to irritated action. He reported to Lord Hillsborough, Secretary of State for the Colonies, that some of the French settlements, specifically Vincennes, attracted undesirables. "Strollers and Vagabonds from Canada, Detroit, Illinois and other Places," he wrote, "have assembled there, to live a lazy kind of Indian life or taken Shelter there from Justice." He described Vincennes, in short, as a "Nest of Villains." Hillsborough lost little time replying and urging that the settlement be dispersed.

On April 8, 1772, General Gage issued the order for dispersal, and it was brought to Vincennes by Captain Hugh Lord, who was commanding in Kaskaskia. Declared General Gage in his proclamation:

> Many persons, contrary to the positive orders of the King upon this subject, have undertaken to make settlements beyond the boundaries fixed by the treaties made with the Indian nations, which boundaries ought to serve as a barrier between the whites and the said nations; and a great number of persons have established themselves, particularly on the river Ouabache, where they lead a wandering life, without government, and without laws, interrupting the free course of trade, destroying the game, and causing infinite disturbance in the country, which occasions a considerable injury to the affairs of the King, as well as to those

of the Indians; His Majesty has been pleased to order, and by these presents orders are given in the name of the King, to all who have established themselves on the lands upon the Ouabache, whether at St. Vincent or elsewhere, to quit this countries instantly and without delay, and to retire, at their choice, into some one of the colonies of His Majesty, where they will be received and treated as the other subjects of His Majesty.[4]

When the citizens of Vincennes had recovered from their shock and dismay—visualizing a fate similar to that of the Acadians—they asked Captain Lord to permit their sending delegates to General Gage to argue against the removal order. Lord sent the French settlers' petition on to Gage, but nothing further was heard of delegates. Instead, the settlers drew up a memorial, with a letter, and sent them on to Gage. Though they were dated September 18, 1772, it was not until the following March that Gage received them, which is an indication of how long it took to communicate to New York from Vincennes.

The British generally were as lax about making the French feel welcome in the colonies as they had been active at buying the Indian allies of the French before the war. General Gage had, in fact, no very clear knowledge of the West. He had had the impression that the area between the Wabash and the Mississippi was fit only for the production of furs and might as well be left to the Indians. He evidently felt that the Indians were easier to deal with than the old French settlers, and he was ignorant of the agricultural possibilities of the area and disinclined to familiarize himself with the remoter reaches under his control.

The letter from the inhabitants of Vincennes contained no fewer than 56 signatures, the memorial one less. The signers represented most, if not all, of the old French families; their names included those of the commandant, Ste. Marie, and the heads of families—Barrois, Cardinal, La Deroute, Bienet, Barellon, Santiez, St. Aubin, Caunaux, Gamelin, Plichon, Latulipe, Millet, Lejeunne, Chabot, Brunet, Villeneuve, Morrin, Denoyen, Lavigne and others.

The letter was brief and succinct. It led off with an expression of injured surprise, and, amid protestations of respect for the General and the King, set forth the assumption that somehow the General had made a mistake—the removal order must have been intended for the vagabonds in Vincennes, it could hardly have been meant for the sturdy citizens who, they pointed out, held possessions based on titles. To obey the order would indeed make them, too, vagabonds, and they accordingly implored General Gage to forward the memorial "to a king we will always be ready to serve to the extent of sacrificing our lives and our property, should this sacrifice be required."

The memorial was somewhat longer. The citizens of Vincennes made clear that their present troubles must rise from greed— that of people who wanted to move in upon their property, and must first blacken them in order to do so. They called upon His Majesty's justice to save them from an unjust order of removal. They could not recognize themselves as meant by the proclamation they had received, and laid claim to having lived in a settlement seventy years old—considerably stretching the term of Vincennes's settlement—which made Vincennes much older than the government of the present King. The removal order made reference to boundary lines and treaties of which the citizens of Vincennes had never heard; if they preceded the "recent peace with France," they could hardly concern Vincennes, for the citizens were not then British subjects; if they followed the peace, the rights of the citizens would surely have been reserved.

They demanded to know what interruption their living in Vincennes had made to the trade. They asked that troops be sent to Vincennes to see for themselves that all was in order in the settlement—that trade was being revived, and that the citizens were useful men. They complained that Vincennes had been neglected, for all that it was important as being the center between Detroit, the Illinois country, and Fort Pitt.

They denied destroying game in the surrounding countryside, pointing out that they hunted to live, just as they had always done—and this only when they were not busy cultivating their fields. This was the pattern of living that maintained throughout the Illinois country, among French, Indians, and even Englishmen. They admitted an inability to do more for the Indians in

and about Vincennes, without more help from a garrison, which
had been denied Vincennes for some time.

Finally, they humbly requested the retraction of the removal
order, not alone for the benefit of the citizens, but for the sake
of the King of England, for, were it carried out, it would serve
the King and his reputation ill, and be held up as an example of
injustice. "It is the nature of the great to take the part of an
unhappy people when justice is on their side." Surely General
Gage could bring himself to withdraw the proclamation and
oblige the inhabitants who had signed the petition.[5]

As General Gage was not by nature readily inclined to change
his mind and shared the perspective of that Colonel Charles
Lawrence, Governor of Nova Scotia, who expelled the Acadians,
the French settlers' expression of confidence in his "superior vir-
tues" might well have been ignored, had it not been for a circumstance they had no part in bringing about. In England, Lord
Hillsborough fell from power and was replaced by Lord Dartmouth, who was less harshly inclined. It was thus to Dartmouth
that Gage forwarded copies of the letter and memorial from
Vincennes, conceding that he could not "decide whether they
are People settled under legal Titles or Strollers who have taken
Land without authority." At the same time, Gage wrote in reply
to the settlers for "a List of all the Settlers, to mention each person by Name, the Date of his Grant, by whom granted, by whom
confirmed, and where it is registered."

Soon after, Gage himself left for England, and his command
passed to General Haldimand, who lost no time in writing to Lord
Dartmouth that the plan to expel the settlers at Vincennes was
not sound, adding that the accounts on which Gage had acted
had proved to be "from Jealous and self-interested Traders."
Haldimand also informed the French at Vincennes that, if they
could prove title to their lands, he would confirm all that were
correct and the king would protect their claims.

The people of Vincennes hastened to obtain affidavits. St. Ange,
who had retreated to the Spanish side of the Mississippi and was
making his home with the Chouteau family at St. Louis, was
appealed to, for he had made some sixty grants during his 28
years at Vincennes. One grant made by Vincennes himself and

confirmed by Governor de Bienville was produced. Grants confirmed by the succeeding governors of French Louisiana—Vaudreuil, Kerlerec, Abadie—were proved by affidavits. Having defeated both the French insistence upon moving the fort to the mouth of the Ohio and the British plan to expel the French from Vincennes, the settlers were thenceforth left alone.

That the indecision regarding the French in the Illinois country and along the Wabash had an effect upon the British government can hardly be denied; partly as a result of it, the Quebec Act of 1774 was passed by Great Britain. It provided for a permanent civil government for Canada, and, in the course of the various provisions of the act, Canada's boundaries were extended to the Ohio River, though the colonies of Virgina, Connecticut and Massachusetts had claims to large areas of that region. Vincennes, long part of the French Province of Louisiana, thus became part of His Britannic Majesty's Province of Canada.

In was not until three years later that the British finally got around to Vincennes. The petitioners who had applied to General Gage to save them from exile had specified their need of a garrison; in May 1777 Lieutenant Governor Edward Abbott came to take command of the fort in Vincennes. Unhappily, he found only the remains of a fort, and nothing that could be called a "fortification" presented itself to his view.

Abbott enlisted the French to build a stockade around his cabin on the site of Vincennes's original fort along the river. Four cannons were sent to him by the commandant at Kaskaskia, Philippe François Rastel, Sieur de Rocheblave. He named his fort after George Sackville, Lord George Germaine, who was then Secretary of State for the American Colonies, and Fort Sackville thereafter took the place of the fort that had been known as "Fort Vincent" or "Fort Vincennes."

But if the inhabitants of Vincennes expected to see a garrison under the British arriving to occupy the post, they were doomed to disappointment. Abbott remained less than a year; frustrated by his failure to obtain from his government the supplies he needed for trade with the Indians—the same complaint Vincennes had made—he left at the beginning of February 1778. Fort Sackville was deserted, and the settlement was without defense.

2

Abbott could hardly have chosen a more ill-advised time to leave Vincennes. Virtually from the time of the passage of the Quebec Act, following as it did the destruction of tea in Boston harbor and the passage of various coercive acts by Parliament in London, the British colonies in America had been in a state of ferment that had soon developed into rebellion and open warfare. During the interval, General Thomas Gage had returned to assume control of British forces, with instructions to put down the insurrection in the colonies. The Continental Congress had been formed, and hostilities had broken out from Bunker Hill north to Canada and south to Fort Moultrie in North Carolina. The Continental Congress had voted a Declaration of Independence, and France, still smarting from its defeat in North America, had been secretly sending munitions to the colonies; it recognized the colonies' independence after the disastrous defeat of General John Burgoyne at Saratoga.

By early 1778 France and the former British colonies in America were in open alliance, and the British, now thoroughly aware of the impasse to which their singular and stubborn arrogance in dealing with the colonies had led them, were making new attempts at conciliation, only to find that the position of the Continental Congress had hardened and that the American colonies were receptive to nothing but the withdrawal of British forces and recognition by England of their independence.

Vincennes had so far been untouched by the revolution, but now the hostilities began to move west. Raiding activities of a band of British, Indians and Loyalists were carried out under the command of Lieutenant Governor Henry Hamilton of Detroit—known as "the Hair-Buyer" because, after holding the Indian allies of the British in restraint for years, he had reversed his policy and sent them to harass the frontier settlements, urging them to bring him scalps. His reversal followed an order from Lord George Germaine, issued in March 1777; after June of that year, Hamilton gave free rein to the Indians.

The Indians, however, had been raiding the Kentucky settlements for some time before the British urged them to do so. Kentucky was then but a county of Virginia, and in Harrodsburg a company of men under the command of John Bowman, a colonel of Virginia, found the settlement under attack by Chief Blackfish and his Shawnee, who laid siege to the settlement. A major in that company of military men was George Rogers Clark, who had not long since held a military commission as "Captain of the Militia of Pittsburg and its Dependencies" and was looked upon as a Virginia soldier with considerable experience in fighting Indians.

Though the Harrodsburg raid had taken place in March—before Lord Germaine's order had been transmitted to the Indians through General Sir Frederick Haldimand, who was commanding in Canada, and Lieutenant Governor Henry Hamilton—it was the catalyst that set in motion countermeasures, for, under siege, Clark concluded that savages, incited and supplied by the British, would only increase their raids if they were not stopped.

He knew very well—as who did not?—that the British were supplying arms to the Indians and that the focus of British power in the Northwest Territory was the fort at Detroit, but he knew very little about the deployment of British forces at the other forts between his position and Detroit, for Clark's ultimate goal was Detroit. Before it could be taken, the forts at Vincennes and Kaskaskia would have to be taken. And before any move could be taken in the direction of Detroit, intelligence about the other forts must be had. Someone would have to spy out the land.

It did not occur to Clark to approach anyone else in authority to implement his plan. He called in men who knew the wilderness and had become accustomed to traveling it. Among them were Simon Kenton and Samuel Moore, Ben Linn and Si Harland; it was not Clark but Kenton who named them in later accounts. He explained that his objective was the Illinois country (as that land area from the Wabash to the Mississippi was known), that he needed to know how many British troops were deployed there, how loyal the French were to the British, what was the total strength of British and French militiamen (presumably now allied to the British as new subjects) and of the Indian allies.

The men drew lots; Samuel Moore and Ben Linn drew the as-

signment, which was to go into the Illinois country and gather
all the information they could without being caught. They were
capable men. Linn knew the Illinois country and had been so
much among the Indians that he could speak Shawnee, Maumee,
Delaware and Kickapoo, all related Algonquian languages. Moore
had had previous experience in spying at Harrodsburg and had
some acquaintance with the Indians. These two set out some
time in the spring of 1777, following the Ohio to the Kaskaskia
River.

In late May they walked into Kaskaskia posing as hunters come
to trade. They were not entirely unexpected, for somehow Clark
had sent word to some of his friends in the area that he would
be dispatching emissaries into Kaskaskia. Among them was a
double agent, Thomas Bentley, who was serving both the Americans and the British. His business associate, Daniel Murray, was
also undoubtedly aware of Clark's purpose in sending his spies
into Kaskaskia. But the easygoing commander, Rocheblave, was
not aware of their purpose and may even have hired them to hunt
meat for his table.

For a while the two spies were free to move about as they
pleased. If the French inhabitants suspected their real purpose,
no one said anything. Rocheblave did not. The Indians in and
around Kaskaskia, however, evidently distrusted Moore and Linn,
and a trader, who had recognized Linn from the Shawnee country
and who concluded that he had come only to spy, warned the
two that the Indians were planning to take some action against
them. Linn and Moore hastily slipped out of Kaskaskia.

By that time, however, they had what they had come for:
They knew that there were no British regulars in the area, either
in Kaskaskia or in Vincennes; that Forts Massac and Chartres had
been abandoned; that the fort at Kaskaskia was not in good condition, for, though there was artillery at the fort, there was no
one to fire it; that there was good reason to believe that the
French could be won over to the American cause, however much
the leading inhabitants, always on the side of the status quo,
professed to be against it; that there was generally more pro-
American than pro-British feeling, though it was seldom given
expression, and that Rocheblave was, however desultorily, stir-

ring up the Indians against the Americans, which was by then official British policy. They reported on the approximate distance of Kaskaskia from Ste. Geneviève (a Spanish village across the Mississippi River, whose people, like those of St. Louis, were decidedly pro-American and anti-British), and they knew the population of the settlement at Kaskaskia. What they did not know, however, was the sentiment of the people of Vincennes or the situation at the fort there, except that there seemed to be no British troops there, as there were none elsewhere in the Illinois country north of the Ohio River and south of Chicago.

Lack of knowledge about Vincennes was not of immediate concern to Clark. His goal was Kaskaskia, which he meant to seize; then he intended to win over not only the French but also the Indians in that region. His plan was a bold one. Failure had dogged attempts launched from Fort Pitt to move down the Ohio into the Illinois country; he did not intend to fail.

It was not a project that he could undertake solely on his own initiative; he needed official sanction. He composed a letter and report on what he had learned and sent it, together with an outline of his plan of attack, to Governor Patrick Henry of Virginia. He followed the report early in December, reaching Williamsburg, the seat of government, at a fortunate time—after Burgoyne's surrender at Saratoga, when a move into the Illinois country seemed advisable to Henry.

Yet it was a bold plan, which gave the Governor pause. Clearly, no hint of Clark's purpose must be permitted to reach the public. It followed that it was too great a risk to lay Clark's proposal before the General Assembly. It was, however, laid before the Governor's Council. Henry's wavering was countered by the support of Thomas Jefferson and George Mason, among others. The Virginia Assembly was asked to approve a force of men, led by Lieutenant Colonel George Rogers Clark—his promotion came with the Governor's decision to approve his plan—to defend the settlements in the County of Kentucky. The governor carefully avoided mentioning that the defense of Kentucky might involve the invasion and attack of the Illinois country.

Clark was authorized to recruit a force of men under arms, and, though recruiting was not easy, he managed to gather somewhat fewer than two hundred men, most of them hardy frontiersmen familiar with the wilderness. A score of families intending to settle west of Virginia elected to go along, for so large an escort would see them through the territory ravaged by the Shawnee. In addition, Clark had the promise of other troops from Kentucky.

The company set out May 12 on the Monongahela, bound for Fort Pitt and Wheeling, where they picked up supplies, and down the Ohio. Clark traveled with two sets of orders. The first commanded him "to proceed, without loss of time, to enlist seven companies of men, officered in the usual manner, to act as militia under your own orders. They are to proceed to Kentucky, and there to obey such orders and directions as you shall give them, for three months after their arrival at that place; but to receive pay, etc., in case they remain on duty a longer time."

His secret orders, also dated January 2, 1778, were somewhat less vague, however; though they began as did the public orders, they went on to order Clark and his company to "attack the British post at Kaskasky. It is conjectured that there are many pieces of Cannon & military Stores to considerable amount at that place, the taking & preservation of which would be a valuable acquisition to the State. If you are so fortunate therefore as to succeed in your Expectation, you will take every possible Measure to secure the artillery & stores & whatever may advantage the State."

Governor Henry was much concerned for the welfare of the settlers:

> It is earnestly desired that you show Humanity to such British Subjects and other persons as fall in your hands. If the white Inhabitants at the post & the neighbourhood will give undoubted Evidence of their attachment to this State (for it is certain they live within its Limits) by taking the Test prescribed by Law and by every other way & means in their power, Let them be treated as fellow Citizens & their persons & property duly secured. Assistance & protection against all Enemies whatever shall be afforded them, & the commonwealth of Virginia is pledged to accomplish it. But if these people will not accede to these reasonable Demands, they must feel the Miseries of War, under the direction of that Humanity that has hitherto distinguished Americans, & which it is expected you will ever consider as the Rule of your Conduct, & from which you are in no Instance to depart.[6]

Clark had no illusions about the daring of his enterprise, but he was undaunted. "I was sensible of the impression it would have on many, to be taken near a thousand miles from the Body of their Country, to attack a People five times their number, and merciless Tribes of Indians their Allies, and determined Enemies to us. I knew that my case was desperate, but the more I reflected on my weakness the more I was pleased with the Enterprize." [7]

Clark and his company moved on past the mouth of the Kentucky River, where he had expected the settlers to remain, taking settlers and all along. On May 27, they reached the Falls of the Ohio—the site of Louisville. Clark had expected four companies to join him there, but there was only half a company of men. Clark immediately sent out a directive to the officers of Kentucky County to send as many men as possible to meet Simon Kenton, his scout, at Drennon's Lick; with Kenton to guide them, they would meet at the Falls.

The settlers were intent upon establishing themselves on an island in the Ohio, where they would be relatively safe from attack, as Clark was keeping his men on the same island for quite another reason—so that desertion would be more difficult—and he finally undertook to read to the company the secret orders he had received from Governor Patrick Henry. He had anticipated that some of his recruits would be dismayed, and so they were; but the majority of them were enthusiastic about the venture, though some were fearful that they were not in sufficient numbers to see the plan through. A vigorous debate between officers and men took place, but the men—perhaps conscious that their commander's ears were everywhere—decided to follow their officers wherever they might lead.

Nevertheless, the greater part of Company A, under the leadership of Lieutenant Thomas Hutchins, who had no stomach for a campaign against the Indians and the British in Illinois, deserted in the night. Clark lost several days in a largely fruitless attempt to track them down, so that it was late June before he and his remaining 178 men were ready to move again. By that time, the men had been turned from raw recruits into reasonably well drilled soldiers inculcated with military discipline.

In four days they reached the Tennessee River, where they encamped on an island. There they were surprised by a party of hunters coming down river. The soldiers put out boats to bring them in and found that the hunters were only eight days out of Kaskaskia. As they were not inimical to Clark's purpose, they conveyed such intelligence as they had to him. It was not minor. Clark learned that Lieutenant Governor Edward Abbott had gone to Detroit, leaving Vincennes virtually undefended. He learned, too, in confirmation of his spies' reports, that, though the French feared the Long Knives, as the Kentuckians were known to them, they were ready to join the Americans if properly handled. As for the Indians' fear, it had been carefully instilled in them by the British, who invariably depicted the savagery of the Kentuckians as far worse than that of the Indians.

The hunters were permitted to go on, and Clark and his company also went on down the Ohio, bound for the ruins of old Fort Massac, which had been abandoned since the Treaty of Paris. They had not yet reached Massac when William Linn, left behind weeks before, caught up with them in a canoe and conveyed a highly important dispatch, informing Clark of the French alliance with the United States. Clark well knew the value of this information as far as the old French settlements of the Illinois country were concerned.

Beyond Massac Clark could not go. By far the easiest route to Kaskaskia would have been from the Mississippi up the Kaskaskia River, for Kaskaskia stood only seven miles from the junction. But the Ohio below the site of Massac was being constantly watched by the British and their allies in the hope of capturing supplies sent from New Orleans or the friendly Spanish settlements west of the Mississippi and destined for the Americans. Clark's route had to be overland, however difficult it would be, and launched from a point from which the British would not be expecting invasion.

Clark ran his boats into the mouth of a small creek a mile above the ruined Fort Massac and concealed them there. After a night's rest, the company began to move northwest, in the direction of Kaskaskia, traveling single file, Indian fashion, in order to be less easily detected. The way led through hilly and wooded country toward open plains and meadows, and Clark later described it as "very fatiguing" in *Campaign in the Illinois.*

The men traveled fifty miles with little rest, but by that time they had come to relatively open country. Clark was somewhat apprehensive that the company might be seen and its approach reported to Kaskaskia. To complicate matters a trifle more, his guide lost his way, and the men wasted several hours before he found it again. But despite tribulations, they moved unseen and by evening of July 4 had reached a point within three miles of Kaskaskia.

They were ready for the attack on the old French capital of the Illinois country. There was no time for delay, and as soon as darkness fell they moved. Their first goal was a farm approximately a mile above Kaskaskia. They took the farmer and his family prisoners and were fortunate enough to find boats in which to cross the river.

Kaskaskia itself lay quiet. This silence was in itself no assurance that the fort had not been warned; armed men and perhaps Indians might be lying in wait for the Virginians. But, however great the danger of ambush, Clark decided to push ahead, all considerations of being outnumbered in battle behind him.

In two hours, Clark and his men were on the other side of the Kaskaskia River. He was quick to plan, quick to execute his plans. The farmer hostage had told him that the Indians, whose villages were not far away, had left Kaskaskia itself, which was good news, for the Indians were never as amenable to reason as were the settlers.

Clark divided his company into two parts, one of which he sent to surround the town. With Simon Kenton and a few picked men, he himself bore down upon the fort, hoping that somehow it could be taken without the firing of a shot to arouse Kaskaskia.

The Commandant, Rocheblave, a French nobleman in unenviable service to the King of England, had asked to be relieved some time before. A former commander at Fort Massac and battle opponent of General Braddock, he believed that an English fort ought to be commanded by an Englishman, particularly as he seemed to win from the British no greater cooperation than the French government had given its posts. Indeed, the British had parsimoniously given him nothing but orders that would have been difficult to carry out under ordinary circumstances and were virtually impossible to execute without men and supplies. To cap their folly, the officials in Canada had even instructed Rocheblave to refrain from sending couriers from Kaskaskia unless the problem were exceedingly grave, and, as General Sir Guy Carleton had sent him no pay, Rocheblave was reduced to running his office at his own expense. He could hardly be blamed for being less than enthusiastic in his defense of Kaskaskia or for the seeming lack of even guards about the fort when Clark and his men approached it.

For, however incredible it was, Clark failed to encounter the armed guard he had expected, or even an Indian scout. His men reached the gates and entered the enclosure. They were not challenged by so much as a sentry. One of the Ohio River hunters who had joined the party pointed out the commander's house, which, like all others in Kaskaskia, was dark and silent. As quietly as possible, Clark and his men invaded it.

Rocheblave and his wife were asleep. They woke to find themselves surrounded by Clark and his ill-kempt, half-starved woodsmen, who must have presented an appearance every bit as terrifying as that of Indians in war paint.

Having secured the fort and its commander, Clark signaled the rest of his little army outside. Immediately, the men sprang into action and "in 15 minutes had every Street secured." Clark then sent through the streets such men under his command as could speak French; they raised the alarm, shouting that Kaskaskia had been taken and ordering the people of the village "on pane of Death" to keep indoors. Before daylight the people of Kaskaskia were disarmed and within doors, fearful of their fate.

Clark wrote in his report:

> Nothing could excell the Confusion these People seemed to be in, being taught to expect nothing but Savage treatment from the Americans. Giving all for lost their Lives were all they could dare beg for, which they did with the greatest fervancy, they were willing to be Slaves to save their Families. I told them it did not suit me to give them an answer at that time, they repared to their houses, trembling as if they were led to Execution; my prin-

cipal would not suffer me to distress such a number of People,
except, through policy, it was necessary.

More than principle was involved. Although it seemed wise to
keep the French settlers in some fear at the outset, it was far from
wise to prolong that fear. Clark knew very well that under the
stress of fear men are likely to take extreme measures for relief.
And he had to think, not only of the Indians nearby, but also of
the posts at Cahokia, some sixty miles above Kaskaskia, and at
Vincennes, more than two hundred miles to the northwest. He
could ill afford to keep the French fearful or even hostile, and
it was, as he put it, "my Interest to Attach them to me."

He sent for the leading citizens of Kaskaskia and, with an air
of injury, told them that he was mortified to learn of their low
opinion of the Americans and their cause. Thereupon he explained
that cause to his captive audience and pointed out that these
conquerors were not in the habit of enslaving people. Rather

> our Principal was to make those we Reduced free insted of en-
> slaving them as they immagined, that if I could have surety of
> their Zeal and Attachment to the American Cause, they should
> immediately enjoy all the priviledges of our Government, and
> their property secured to them, that it was only to stop the farther
> effusion of Innocent Blood by the Savages under the influence of
> their Governour, that made them an object of our attention.

The French, understandably, were relieved and grateful. They
explained that they had never been informed of the basis of the
quarrel between the Americans and the British and that they had,
on the other hand, always heard frightful tales of the savagery of
the Big Knives. Clark told them that an oath of fidelity was all
that was required of the citizens, adding that they could take
time to think about it; he would not administer the oath for several days, and in the meantime any settler who did not wish to
swear loyalty to the Americans was free to leave with his family.

Among the men thus summoned before Clark was the local
priest, Father Pierre Gibault, who had been sent from Canada
by his Jesuit superiors in 1768. He had remained in Kaskaskia
after the summer of that year, and in the following year he braved

hostile Indians to reach Vincennes, which was also in his charge. He was thus familiar with the settlement and at the same time somewhat more informed of the course of the American Revolution. He was also profoundly in sympathy with the Americans, though for the nonce he held his counsel and asked permission only to continue his office, which, Clark assured him, there was no wish to interrupt.

Cahokia was the next goal. Obviously, it would not do to let too much time elapse before marching upon that settlement, lest word of the invasion reach the citizenry in time to allow them to prepare a defense. Even before moving, Clark thought it necessary to be certain of the attitude of the Spanish on the west bank of the Mississippi, and he sent Levi Todd across the Mississippi to Ste. Geneviève. Todd was instructed to spy out information on how many men under arms and how much artillery there were, and to learn, if possible, the Spanish attitude toward the Americans.

Meanwhile, Clark prepared to advance on Cahokia; he meant to send a detachment of his men under the command of Captain Joseph Bowman, who was to command at Cahokia after its capitulation. The French settlers at Kaskaskia, however, interposed some objections. Why expose anyone to battle when they, if they were permitted to do so, might go instead to Cahokia and inform the French there of what had taken place? They had not a moment of doubt that Cahokia would gladly receive and swear loyalty to the Americans.

Clark was not fully persuaded, but he allowed himself to commit only Captain Bowman to the journey to Cahokia. After all, the whole of Kaskaskia was hostage to the French settlers' failure. Bowman left Kaskaskia for Cahokia posing as one of the French inhabitants who had chosen to go on the mission and indistinguishable from them.

Bowman and the inhabitants, all in frontier clothes, rode into Cahokia after traversing the fifty-odd miles between Kaskaskia and that town and simply announced their purpose. Indeed, the French from Kaskaskia did all the talking, and the French in Cahokia were receptive. The only townsmen who took a dim view were the Indians. "A number of Indians being in Town, on hearing of the Big Knives, immediately made their Escape." The

French in Cahokia, given—like those in Kaskaskia—a few days to think over a change of loyalties, presently took the oath of loyalty to the Americans. The Kaskaskia French returned to Clark with a message from Bowman, and Bowman took over the settlement of Cahokia, as ordered.

And presently Levi Todd returned from the Spanish lands. He had been arrested at Ste. Geneviève, but then, upon the Spaniards' learning what had happened in the Illinois country, he had been feted. He had visited St. Louis, knew all about the disposal of Spanish arms and forces and had discovered that the Spanish, themselves on the verge of war with Great Britain and well aware of the new alliance between France and the Americans, made no secret of their preference for the American cause. Indeed, Señor Don Fernando de Leyba, Lieutenant Governor at St. Louis, so expressed himself in a letter to Clark.

Clark had secured most of the Illinois country. With the Spanish on his side, even though only passively, he did not have to worry about attack from the west. The Indians, however, and Vincennes remained. Vincennes was a pocket of possible trouble; he knew too little of it. Two hundred forty miles separated it from Kaskaskia, and, though its British commander had gone to Detroit, it was possible that British soldiers had taken command during the interval while Clark and his men were taking Kaskaskia and Cahokia. Vincennes was the only other large settlement in the Illinois country.

Though by that time the Indians in the vicinity of the captured posts knew what was taking place—and soon, too, the British at Detroit would know—word of the capture of Kaskaskia and Cahokia had certainly not yet reached Vincennes. Before advancing upon that post, Clark had to know all he could about its defenses. In any case, his men were spread thin, and he would soon be hard put to bluff much longer. In short, detaching a force for Vincennes would leave him dangerously exposed to those Indians whom he had not yet taken the trouble to win over.

He fell back upon his customary tactic; he chose to send Simon Kenton, Shadrach Bond and Elisha Batty to learn who and how many men manned the fort at Vincennes. They set off without delay, careful to avoid meeting anyone. Nearing Vincennes, they traveled by night, and, once at the settlement, they hid in the woods and watched the town.

After most of a day's observation, they wrapped themselves in blankets and walked unchallenged into Vincennes. No one paid any attention to them. They went wherever they liked and found no sign of any suspicion among the inhabitants. Vincennes was still unaware of what had happened at Kaskaskia and Cahokia. And, most astonishing to Clark's spies, though the British commander was clearly gone, there was neither a force of regular troops nor any armed militiamen. Nor was there any sign of warlike Indians. Vincennes apparently lay open to attack and capture, though there was no way of knowing how many Indians would be roused to its defense should a body of armed men proceed from Kaskaskia, for so large a group could not hope to go unseen for a great distance along a route traveled by hunters and traders.

But Clark did not wait for a report from Vincennes. He noised it about that he intended to attack Vincennes and made bluffing talk of having more troops ready at the Falls of the Ohio. He was fishing for reactions from the French at Kaskaskia. It was not slow in coming.

Father Pierre Gibault came to Clark's quarters. He said bluntly in his gentle way that there was no need to risk spilling blood by an attack on Vincennes; its citizens were, he assured Clark, as interested in changing sides as those of Kaskaskia had been. True, they needed some preparation. Father Gibault offered to go to Vincennes himself and, as Clark put it, "win that Town for me if I would permit him and let a few of them go; they made no doubt of gaining their friends at St. Vincents to my Interest; the Priest told me he would go himself, and gave me to understand, that although he had nothing to do with temporal business, that he would give them such hints in the Spiritual way, that would be very conducive to the business." [8]

Clark was convinced of the priest's genuine concern for the interests of the Americans. But Father Gibault could not go alone, though Clark provided him with a horse. The priest suggested that Dr. Jean Baptiste Laffont, who had, like himself, served both Kaskaskia and Vincennes, go along. Both men were trusted by the people of Vincennes. A few other French settlers of Kaskaskia proposed to go with them and to add their persuasiveness in the American cause.

Clark prepared a proclamation for them to carry to Vincennes, to be produced when the temper of the citizens was known. Then he turned his attention to other matters while waiting out the weeks it would take before the party could return from the country of the Wabash.

He did not once lose sight of the fact that, despite the newly declared loyalty of the French, he had under his command a total of fewer than the 200 men with whom he had started out—fewer by that half-company that had deserted with Lieutenant Hutchins. Furthermore, all the remaining men had enlisted for a period of only three months, and their time of enlistment was coming to an end. It would make a very bad impression on the French if his little army were suddenly depleted.

He began to exercise all his powers of persuasion to keep his men. If all went well, Simon Kenton, he knew, would follow instructions and would be on his way to Colonel John Bowman at Harrodsburg with a report and a request for more men, but the enlistment time would have passed long before a reply could be expected in the Illinois country. Exceeding his authority, he promised his men presents and advances in pay, thereby convincing a hundred of them to stay. Those who elected to return were sent off as a guard for Rocheblave, who was being taken as a prisoner to the East; these men were presumably to be replaced by others from the Falls or from Virginia.

Clark turned next to the problem of the Indians. He had been giving some thought to winning them as allies. He needed to do so. He had not nearly enough men to engage them successfully in battle, though neither the French nor the Indians were aware of this fact. Clark did his best, by constant bluffing references to the army waiting to be called upon, to keep them from finding out. He decided finally, after having prepared the way with rumors and exaggerations, to take the Indians by the same kind of bold conduct with which he had allied the French to the American cause.

He invited all the Indians within reach to meet with the Big

Knives in council at Cahokia. By that time the reputation of the red-headed Clark was widespread and considerably inflated, which Clark himself did his best to further. The puzzled Indians, knowing that their British allies were far away, hardly knew what to do, but each application for advice to the French traders was answered the same way: Deal with the Americans.

Clark knew very well that conciliatory talk was lost on the Indians, who respected only strength. He was prepared to bluster. Meeting with the great council at Cahokia—and the numbers of Indians who had come, representing Ojibwa, Winnebago, Iowa, Sauk, Fox, Potawatomi, Ottawa, Miami and others, astonished even Clark, though he did not show it—he acted as if the Indians' presence was a natural tribute to him, and he spoke to them harshly, as a conqueror against whose forces they could not hope to mount a successful attack. Once they were filled with apprehension, he saw fit to explain the war between the British and the Americans in a highly colored address.

> A great many Years ago, our forefathers lived in England, but the King oppressed them in such a manner that they were obliged to Cross the great Waters to get out of his way. But he not being satisfied to loose so many subjects sent Governours and Soldiers among them to make them obey his Laws, but told his Governours to treat them well and to take but little from them until they grew Populus, that then they would be able to pay a great deal. By the good treatment we got, we grew to be a great People and flourished fast. The King then wrote to his Governour & Officers that we had got Rich and numerous enough, that it was time to make us pay tribute, that he did not care how much they took, so as they left us enough to eat, and that he had sent them a great many Soldiers to make the Americans pay if they refused, that when they had made the Americans do as they pleased, they would then make the Indians pay likewise; But for fear the Indians should find it out by the Big Knives, that the English intended to make them also pay, & should get mad with the English for their treatment of their Neighbours the Big Knives, that they, his Governours, should make us quarrel, &c. We bore their Taxes for many Years, at last they were so hard that if we killed a Deer they would take the Skin away and leave us the Meat, and made us buy Blankets with Corn to fead their soldiers with. But such

usage we got Poor and was obliged to go naked; And at last we complained. The King got mad and made his Soldiers Kill some of our People and Burn some of our Villages. The Old Men then held a great Council and made the Tomahawk very sharp and put it into the hand of the Young Men, told them to be strong & Strike the English as long as they could find one on this Island. They immediately struck and Killed a great many of the English. The French King hearing of it sent to the Americans and told them to be strong and fight the English like Men, that if they wanted help or Tomahawks he would furnish them. . . .

Clark knew very well that wartime propaganda, however exaggerated, was effective. "This speech had a greater effect than I could have immagined, and did more service than a Regiment of Men cou'd have done."

He did not want for courage in the face of singularly great odds. When some Winnebago made an attempt to kidnap him, he immediately ordered the Winnebago chieftains, who knew nothing of the rash attempt planned by some of the braves, to be put in irons. The Indians concluded that only a leader who had unlimited numbers of men at his command would dare take such measures. He wrote in retrospect:

To shew the Indians that I disregarded them, I remained in my Lodging in the Town, about one hundred Yards from the Fort seemingly without a Guard, but I kept about fifty Men conceiled in a Parlour adjoining, and the Garrison under Arms; there was great Counciling among the Savages dureing the Night. But to make them have the greater idea of my Indifferency about them, I assembled a Number of Gentlemen & Ladies, and danced nearly the whole Night.

At the council the following morning, after Clark had made a bold speech offering the Indians either peace or war, the chiefs of the various tribes eagerly sought peace. Though Clark was under no illusions, knowing that Indian allies could be bought by whoever offered the highest rewards, he had for the time being separated the Indians from the British, who would now have to approach them and make fresh representations, which would consume valuable time.

To cap his triumph, Father Gibault and Dr. Laffont returned from Vincennes to say that the inhabitants of that post were all for joining the Americans in their cause against the British. Even the local militia, which had been serving the British, however desultorily, was quite prepared to defend Vincennes for the Americans.

Clark's delight was tempered by his knowledge that the militia could as readily turn coat again at the appearance of an enemy force. It was thus necessary to garrison Fort Sackville, to have control of the cannon and other weapons at that fort. He chose from among his men Captain Leonard Helm, a seasoned Indian fighter, to command the fort and sent him with a small force of men—perhaps a score—to Vincennes. His conquest of the Illinois country between Virginia and the Mississippi and south of Chicago was complete.

3

Within a month the British at Detroit were fully informed about Clark's conquest. Francis Maisonville, a boatwright from Detroit who lived among other hunters and traders in the Illinois country and who was appreciably more devoted to the British than were many other men in that country, had made careful note of all that Clark had accomplished—though Clark had still not had his success with the Indians. At the time that Father Gibault and Dr. Laffont were setting out for Vincennes, Maisonville sent a summary of what he had learned to Detroit.

The news reached Governor Henry Hamilton at an ill moment. Hamilton had been gathering arms and men for the implementing of a dream of his own: the seizure of Fort Pitt. He now saw that he would have to abandon his dream temporarily, for, if he did not, Clark might well march his army up and take Detroit. Hamilton's spy, like most of the inhabitants of the Illinois country, had been taken in by Clark's extraordinary boldness and had believed the story that a considerable body of troops waited at the Falls of the Ohio. With the replacement of Sir Guy Carleton by Major General Sir Frederick Haldimand as commander and Governor of Canada, Hamilton's dream of capturing Fort Pitt was doomed in any event, for Haldimand knew that, even if the British could take Fort Pitt, they could not supply it.

Hamilton determined to move at once, meanwhile sending out agents to spy in advance of his coming. It seemed to him logical, if Clark were at Kaskaskia, to strike at Vincennes and thus to cut him off from direct help from the Americans east of the Wabash. He could use the munitions and men assembled for his planned assault on Fort Pitt.

Once Vincennes was in his hands, Hamilton could take his time closing in on Clark from the east while the Indian allies of the British came in from the west. He did not yet know the extent of the disaffection Clark had wrought among the Indians.

He wrote a full account of what he proposed to do and dispatched it to Quebec. On October 7, "having received His Excellency's permission," [9] he led a compact army down the Erie from Detroit by boat, sending a supply train laden with provisions by land to the Miami. In a letter to Lord Shelburne later, Hamilton wrote that his force consisted of "One Lieutenant fireworker, two Matrosses with one six pounder one Lieutenant, 2 Sarjeants, 30 rank and file of the 8th Regt., one Captain, one Lieut., 3 Serjeants, 40 private Volunteers, Two Captains, 4 Lieuts., 60 private volunteer Militia, Seventy Indians with their Officers and Interpreters. We had not craft for greater numbers, having to transport 97,000 pounds weight of Provisions, ammunition & stores." [10] He expected to find at or near Vincennes some 350 Indians who had been allies of the British during the time they had held Vincennes. He expected, too, to gather more Indians along the way down the Wabash to his goal.

Hamilton's artillery served him well. Wherever he stopped, he paused to sit in council with the Indians. He smoked the peace pipe with Miami, Chippewa, Shawnee, Kickapoo, Ottawa and others. To impress them even more, he fired a shot from his artillery now and then. He could hit a target three hundred yards away. The Indians, who by that time knew that Clark had so far shown no such weapon, were indeed impressed and perfectly willing to ally themselves to any side that had such powerful arms. Hamilton himself sang the Indians' war songs, which almost convinced the Indians that he was one of their own.

Hamilton pushed through the now wintry countryside at his own pace, pausing where he liked. Major Jehu Hay, a Detroit officer with his company and much hated by the Virginians because of his success at stirring up the Indians against them, was particularly active with spies. From Lake Erie, up the Maumee to a nine-mile portage, to a tributary of the Wabash they went, much delayed by the necessity of moving the six-pounder that so impressed the Indians.

At Ouiatenon, among friendly Indians, Hamilton was told that Vincennes was under the command of Lieutenant Helm and that Clark himself remained in Kaskaskia. Hamilton reasonably concluded that the main force under Clark was with him and not at Vincennes. He did not foresee any difficulty in taking and holding Fort Sackville.

He moved steadily down the Wabash but with as much care as if he were going to engage a major force. He sent scouting parties ahead, for he was certain that Lieutenant Helm would be maintaining some reconnaissance.

So he was. Lieutenant Helm, a bibulous fellow in his fifties, somewhat handicapped by an injured right arm, had indeed been sending out spies, certain that the British must inevitably strike back and perhaps as aware as Hamilton that Vincennes, from a military point of view, was the logical goal for the initial offensive to regain the Illinois country. He could have no knowledge of how much the British knew of the size of Clark's force or of his own defenses at Vincennes. And he was handicapped by an insufficiency of good scouts; he had to fall back upon the Vincennes militia.

Hamilton, as he and his army neared Vincennes, found increasing traces of people nearby—a fire left burning on a raft, the tracks of horses—and he laid traps for Helm's scouts, though none was effective. In mid-December, however, a scouting party captured Lieutenant Michel Brouillet and three men of the Vincennes militia.

Lieutenant Brouillet, who carried commissions in both the American and the British forces, mollified Hamilton's sense of outrage at this cavalier disregard for the formalities of warfare by proving as talkative as he was cavalier. Perhaps the looming possibility of torture by the Indian allies of the British, who were never averse to a little cruel fun, loosened his tongue. At any rate, Hamilton learned that Lieutenant Helm depended on the French militia, that the people were all in their homes and, in short, that Vincennes was without anything approaching an adequate defense.

Hamilton prepared to take Vincennes. He laid his plans with professional skill. Before the assault could be made, if it proved necessary, Vincennes must be cut off from any possible help. Indians were sent to "lay upon the roads at some distance from the fort to intercept any messengers who might be dispatched to carry intelligence to the Illinois, or to the Falls of Ohio, where a Fort had lately been erected, and an establishment of American settlers had been formed. . . ." [11]

Despite Hamilton's reputation for brutality, he made every effort to prevent slaughter at Vincennes. Major Jehu Hay impressed the old chiefs among their allies that there must be no atrocities if the settlers surrendered. Then, at Hamilton's order, he and the chiefs were sent into Vincennes. In addition to keeping the roads under surveillance, he made sure that both approaches from the river were secured; if Hay's information was correct, how could Lieutenant Helm do anything other than surrender? There was always, however, the chance that Hay had been misinformed, and Hamilton did not intend to risk anything on that chance.

Major Hay went into Vincennes without impediment and immediately went about his business of persuading the French settlers to change sides again and to turn in their arms. The French were willing enough—anything to prevent carnage.

Meanwhile, Hamilton moved down the Wabash toward Vincennes after Hay. Catching up with him, Hamilton learned that the French were renewing their loyalty to Great Britain. There would therefore be no trouble about the village of Vincennes. The fort remained. But Hamilton was ready to counter any action Lieutenant Helm might take.

For his part, Helm had been expecting the arrival of the British for some time. Scouts had come in with the news that a British party was coming from the north, but none brought Helm any specifics. He knew no more than that there were redcoats and Indians, nothing of their number. He could guess at their purpose. By that time, he also knew of the French renewal of loyalty to Great Britain. And he knew very well that he could not possibly defend Fort Sackville.

At the moment of Hamilton's approach to Vincennes, Helm was hastily writing a letter to Clark:

> Dr. Sir—At this time there is an army within three miles of this place. I heard of their comin several days before hand, I sent spies to find the certainty [the scouting party under Lieutenant Brouillet, whose failure to return was indication enough of enemy action], the spies being taken prisoners, I never got intelligence till they got within 3 miles of the town, as I had called the militia & had all assurance of their integrity I order, at the fireing of a Cannon, every man to appear, but I saw but few. Capt. Buseron behaved much to his honour & credit but I doubt the certainty of a certain gent. Excuse haste as the army is in sight. My determination is to defend the Garrison though I have but 21 men but wh't has lef me. I referr you to Mr. Wm. for the rest. The army is in three hunred y'd of village. You must think how I feel, not four men that I can really depend on, but am determined to act brave; think of my condition I know its out of my power to defend the town as not one of the militia will take arms thoug before sight of the army no braver men than. Their flag is at a small distance. I must conclud. . . .[12]

Helm's messenger slipped out of Vincennes on the road to Kaskaskia only moments before Governor Hamilton chose to advance upon Fort Sackville, preceded by the six-pounder aimed at the gate and a detachment of regular troops from the King's Regiment. With the field gun in position, Hamilton sent a man to demand the presence of the commanding officer of Fort Sackville.

Standing on his dignity, Helm demanded to know who summoned him. Told that Hamilton was at the wicket of the fort gate, Helm sent to learn what terms of surrender Hamilton offered. Hamilton did not lose patience; it was supremely important to hold the Indians in check, and the young braves were always impulsive and hotheaded. He promised Helm all that he could promise: that he would be treated with humanity and so would his men, who numbered not 21, as Helm had written Clark, but only three Virginians.

The wicket was opened, and, though the Indians, eager to seize the horses inside the fort and to loot the buildings there, crawled through the portholes and followed Hamilton through the wicket, Helm himself was confined to quarters and guarded by sentries posted by Hamilton.

While the Indians rode off in all directions on the horses they had caught inside the stockade, which Hamilton was powerless to prevent lest he bring about the very slaughter he desired to prevent, the scouts watching the trace to Kaskaskia and Cahokia brought in Helm's mounted messenger and the feverish dispatch Helm had written to Clark; Clark would thus have no intelligence of what had happened to Fort Sackville.

Hamilton was not impressed by what he found in the way of fortifications at Vincennes. "In this miserable picketted work called a fort," he wrote in his *Journal*, "was found scarce anything for defense, the want of a well was sufficient to evince its being untenable—two Iron three pounders mounted on truck carriages and two Swivels not mounted constituted its whole defence, for there were not even platforms for small arms, nor men to use them, the Company of rascal volunteers, 70 in number, having to a man deserted on our approach, and left Captain Helm with only three Virginians for a Garrison."

Hamilton's capture of Fort Sackville and Vincennes had been as bloodless as he had hoped it might be. He was not concerned about Clark or Clark's reaction because he was confident that, by the time Clark did learn that the fort had again changed hands, he would be unable to do anything about it until summer once again cleared the low areas of the spring floods. It was already past mid-December, and Hamilton entertained a firm hope of taking Clark himself prisoner before Clark could be ready to move against Vincennes—if he were rash enough to try it.

The victorious commander, once in possession of the fort, could afford to let his Indian allies go. "The Indians had to return (some of them) 700 miles, to plant corn for their families in the

Spring, and could not be kept together much longer," he wrote in his report and apologia to Lord Shelburne.

Lieutenant Helm remained Hamilton's prisoner, but the two men soon became very friendly, once Helm had promised not to escape and not to try to communicate in any way with Kaskaskia or the Americans at any other point. He had the freedom of the fort and was not kept from knowledge of what Hamilton was planning—to undo the work of Clark among the Indians and ally them once more to Great Britain, to fortify Fort Sackville, to build barracks, to sink a well and to continue to send out parties seeking intelligence of the Americans and their activities on all fronts, but most particularly Kaskaskia, where Clark maintained his headquarters.

All the approaches to Vincennes were kept under continuous surveillance, though travelers between distant points in the Illinois country were few in midwinter. Yet one day Lieutenant Quindre and his force returned to the fort with two prisoners: a Canadian trader named Antoine Renaud and an Italian resident of St. Louis (and thus a Spanish citizen) named Francis Vigo.

Vigo was a merchant who had traveled to Kaskaskia some time before particularly to offer Clark such assistance as he could, which meant not only the use of his not inconsiderable influence but monetary assistance as well. He knew how lax distant governments could be in supporting their colonials, and the government of Virginia was no exception. Though his headquarters were in St. Louis, where he was on intimate terms and in business partnership of a sort with Governor Leyba, he made frequent trips to Kaskaskia.

On one such trip he learned of Clark's uneasiness about the situation in Vincennes, for no word had come from that post to Kaskaskia since Hamilton had taken it. He promptly volunteered his services, and his presence in Vincennes was the direct result of Clark's acceptance of those services. Vigo, captured, kept his wits about him.

Hamilton questioned him at the fort. Vigo was not hesitant in his answers. Indeed, he affected considerable scorn for the Americans, belittling them and suggesting that Clark's troops were without discipline, that they were not adequately deployed, that, in fact, they ran at large through Kaskaskia and Cahokia. This news was welcome to Hamilton, for the conquest of Kaskaskia and the capture of Clark were made to seem more possible than ever.

Hamilton could think of no good reason to keep Vigo prisoner. Anyone else—French, Indian or American—who came within reach of Vincennes could be held and was; but Vigo was a Spanish citizen, and relations between Spain and Great Britain were touchy enough without aggravating them. He made Vigo promise that he would not pause at Kaskaskia and give information to the Americans while on his way to St. Louis. Vigo gave his word.

He was freed to go on about his business in Vincennes. He went out and moved about the settlement at will, filling himself with information. When he had finished, he returned as rapidly as possible to St. Louis and then immediately turned around and started for Kaskaskia and Clark. He had thus not broken his word to Hamilton; he had not paused to inform Clark on his way to St. Louis, but he delayed not a moment thereafter.

"In the hight of our anxiety on the evening of the 29th of Jany, 1779, Mr. Vague, a Spanish mercnt, arrived from St. Vincents, and . . . gave me every intiligence that I could wish to have," recalled Clark not long after his campaign had ended.[13] Vigo proved to be a far better observer than one of the frontier woodsmen might have been, in this instance. "We got Every Information from this Gentn that we could wish for."

Of primary importance to Clark, Vigo reported that most of Hamilton's Indians had gone back to their homes but expected to join Hamilton again in time for the spring campaign against Kaskaskia. During the winter, therefore, Hamilton's strength, however well disciplined—for Hamilton, a onetime captain of His Majesty's Fifteenth Foot, was devoted to discipline—would be at its lowest. Of the people at Vincennes, Vigo was inclined to believe that most would change sides as readily as they had done twice before, that they all wanted an end to the suspense, settlement of the situation one way or another—preferably by Americans.

Clark immediately recognized his situation as critical. Those

Indians still with Hamilton, some of them unquestionably Shawnee, were guarding the Ohio River, intent upon cutting off Kaskaskia from any contact with the government of Virginia, whereas
Hamilton himself was pressing his plan to unite the Indians of
Illinois with those to the south, a plan that, if it could be successfully concluded, would bring such a force under arms against the
Americans that not only Illinois but Kentucky also would fall to
the British. And before a sufficient force could be aroused against
the British, Virginia east of Kentucky County might also be under
attack.

If Clark and his ragged little army were to stay where they
were, they would face certain defeat once spring came, no matter
how thoroughly they fortified their position; they could not hold
out against the large force that Hamilton would be able to bring
against them. Furthermore, each day that Hamilton remained in
control of Vincennes strengthened his position among the Indians
and weakened Clark's.

The alternative was only slightly less grim. If Hamilton thought
that he was safe in Vincennes for the winter, it was left to Clark
to prove him wrong. There was nothing for Clark to do but
attack Vincennes, though the country between Kaskaskia and
Vincennes was all bog and ice-covered water. He put the proposal
to his men:

> I considered the Inclemency of the season, the badness of the
> Roads, &c., as an advantage to us, as they would be more off
> their Guard on all Quarters. I collected the Officers, told them the
> probability I thought there was of turning the scale in our favour.
> I found it the sentiment of every one of them and eager for it.[14]

Clark lost no time. He sent to Cahokia for Captain McCarty
and his men and made ready to transport his weapons and
supplies.

> I had a Large Boat prepared and Rigged, mounting two four
> pounders 4 large swivels Manned with a fine Comp. commanded
> by Lieut. Rogers. She set out in the evening of the 4th of Feby.
> with orders to force her way if possible within ten Leagues of
> St. Vincents and lay until further Orders. This Vessell when com-
> pleat was much admired by the Inhabitants as no such thing had

been seen in the Country before. I had great Expectations from
her. I conducted myself as though I was sure of taking Mr. Hamilton, instructed my officers to observe the same Rule. In a day
or two the Country seemed to believe it, many anctious to Retrieve their Characters turned out, the Ladies began also to be
spirited and interest themselves in the Expedition, which had
great effect on the Young Men.[15]

On the following day Clark and his men began their march.
Captain Richard McCarty came from Cahokia with his Company, Captain François Charleville raised a company of militia
in Kaskaskia but, by the time in midafternoon that the men were
ready to march, there were, counting the 46 men on the boat,
which Clark had named *Willing*, "only a little upwards of two
hundred."

Clark was confident:

I cannot account for it but I still had inward assurance of success, and never could when weighing every Circumstance doubt
it: But I had some secret check. We had now a Rout before us
of two hundred and forty miles in length, through, I suppose, one
of the most beautiful Country in the world, but at this time in
many parts flowing with water and exceading bad marching.

In the company, Captain Joseph Bowman kept a journal of
the historic march. "About 3 o'clock we crossed the Kaskaskia
with our baggage and marched about a league from town. Fair
and drizzly weather. Began our march early. Made a good march
for about nine hours, the road very bad, with mud and water."
On February 8: "Marched early through the waters, which we
now began to meet in those large and level plains, where, from
the flatness of the country, rests a considerable time before it
drains off." On February 10: "Crossed the river of the Petit Fork
upon trees that were fell for that purpose. The water being so
high there was no fording it,—still raining and no tents—encamped
near the river. Stormy weather." [16]

Rain, cold, water and mud were the aspects of the journey
that Captain Bowman recorded most often. Now and then there
was a note of fatigue. On February 12: "The road very bad from

the immense quantity of rain that had fallen. The men much fatigued." On that day, though, they had killed some buffalo and presumably had fresh meat.

Rain fell on every third day of the march; it was not conducive to ease or comfort in marching. The men were wet and exhausted from marching through various depths of water, sometimes with only arms, heads and guns out of the water. Their most important problem was keeping their powder dry. Clark and his officers did their utmost to keep up the morale of the men, but the route grew increasingly difficult.

On February 13 they met with what Clark called "the first obstruction of any consequence."

> Arriveing at the two little Wabachees although three miles asunder they now make but one, the flowed water between them being at Least three feet deep, and in many places four: Being near five miles to the opposite Hills, the shallowest place, except about one hundred Yards, was three feet. This would have been enough to have stoped any set of men that was not in the same temper that we was.[17]

It took the company three days to cross. And then it was only "by building a large Canoe, ferried across the two Channels, the rest of the way we waded; Building scaffolds at each to lodge our Baggage on until the Horses Crossed to take them." In one more day, on the evening of February 17, the exhausted army reached the Embarrass River. It was close enough to Vincennes to hear the gun at Fort Sackville, but the river was forbidding, and there was still the Wabash itself ahead.

"We found it deep in water, it being nine miles to St. Vincents, which stood on the East side of the Wabash and every foot of the way covered with deep water." They marched down the Embarrass, in order to reach the bank of the Wabash. Once they were there, they "made a small Canoe" and sent down river to learn whether the *Willing* had reached its position and to "hurry it up." "From the spot we now lay on was about ten miles to Town, and every foot of the way put together that it was not three feet and upwards under water would not have made the length of two miles and half, and not a mouthful of Provision; to have waited for our Boat, if possible to avoid it, would have been Impolitic." [18]

The march to that point was an incredible feat, as Clark himself viewed it in retrospect; but at the moment the compulsion to victory was so strong that it pushed them through obstacles of even so discouraging a kind. On February 18 Captain Bowman recorded in his journal: "made rafts for four men to cross and go up to town and steal boats. But they spent day and night in the water to no purpose, for there was not one foot of dry land to be found." On February 19: "Capt. McCarty's company set to making a canoe; and at 3 o'clock the four men returned after spending the night on some old logs in the water. . . . No provisions of any sort, now two days. Hard fortune!" Rain added to their misery. Some of the men, "particularly the volunteers," were discouraged and "much cast down"; Clark did his utmost to cheer them up, exhorting them to keep their spirits and their courage, for they would soon be dry and fed and among friends. But on February 22 Captain Bowman still mentioned the lack of food: "No provisions yet. Lord help us!"

They had a little more than courage and luck in their cause. They had taken a party of Frenchmen from Vincennes prisoner, and Captain Willings' brother, who had been a prisoner at Fort Sackville, had made his escape and found Clark's army. They were therefore in possession of major intelligence about Hamilton's position. Clark knew that his coming was unsuspected; Hamilton was so confident that no army would venture to march against Fort Sackville under such conditions that he had relaxed his vigilance. The French in Vincennes were unhappy with the discipline of the British and ready, as always, to change sides. It was evident to Clark that Hamilton "was able to defend himself for a considerable time, but knew that he was not able to turn out of the Fort for lack of a sufficient force of dependable men." But the information he had received suggested that, if Hamilton were permitted to hold out too long, "a Superior number might come against us, as I knew there was a Party of English not far above in the River; that if they found out our Numbers might raise the disaffected Savages and harrass us."

Clark's forces were facing Horseshoe Plain; or at least in ordinary weather it was a plain. It was now a lake "about four miles long, all covered with water breast high," as Bowman saw it. "Here we expected some of our brave men must certainly perish, having froze in the night, and so long fasting." The plain had to be crossed, however, water or not. Clark led the way, plunging into the water with his gun held high. Those men who were too weak or numb with cold went into the few boats. Despite some unhappiness at the conditions of the march, their spirits were high. "Never were men so animated with the thought of avenging the wrongs done to their back settlements, as this small army was." [19]

Early in the afternoon of February 23 they came within sight of Vincennes and halted on Warren's Island, which was, happily, dry. There they captured a prisoner, a Frenchman from Vincennes who was out hunting ducks. He proved to be friendly and assured Clark that no one in the fort or in the settlement had the least intimation of the presence of the Americans. Clark decided to free the captive and send back to Vincennes with him a letter to be circulated among the inhabitants.

> Gentlemen:—Being now within two miles of your village with my army, determined to take your Fort this night, and not being willing to surprise you, I take this method to request such of you as are true citizens, and willing to enjoy the liberty I bring you, to remain still in your houses. And those, if any there be, that are friends to the King, will instantly repair to the fort and join the Hair-buyer General, and fight like men. And if any such, as do not go to the Fort shall be discovered afterwards, they may depend on severe punishment. On the contrary, those that are true friends to liberty, may depend on being well treated. And I once more request them to keep out of the streets; for every one I find in arms on my arrival, I shall treat as an enemy.[20]

All that afternoon the men lay in the sunlight, drying themselves. Time was necessary, in any event, for the letter to be circulated in the village. Their position was fortunately out of sight of the fort because houses intervened. The letter itself was a masterpiece of bravado; Clark meant it to be so and expected that its challenge would bias the French in his favor and frighten into silence those among them who were not for the Americans.

Furthermore, the impression given the duck hunter was that Clark had at least a thousand men prepared to advance upon Vincennes. This impression was in keeping with his policy of boldness and bluff, courage and daring; he used every ruse and deception to sustain that policy, notably the flaunting of many standards in the colors of Virginia on high poles when the men marched behind the knolls obliquely away from Vincennes. The number of men was thus concealed—but it was far smaller than the number of standards suggested to the watcher. Nor had he claimed to have come from Kaskaskia, for he recognized that the march he and his men had made was so difficult that it was more credible to say simply that they had marched up from Kentucky, which also implied the likelihood that a supporting force was not far away; it was the same ruse that had been so successful at Kaskaskia.

Soon it was evening of February 23. Such activity as Clark and his observers had been able to see in Vincennes through the glasses they carried suggested that the villagers were thoroughly aroused and aware but that there was no corresponding activity at the fort. There was nothing but the sound of the evening gun, no rolling of drums to sound alarm, no movement in and out of the fort to suggest any increase in the normal activity of the fort. With the coming of evening, Clark ceased the marching of his troops—the same troops—around and around a knoll to heighten the deception as to the number of men with him. The little army prepared to move upon Vincennes and Fort Sackville, with Captain John Williams, Captain Edward Worthington and Captain François Charleville's companies in the lead, forming the first division, and Captain Joseph Bowman and Captain Richard McCarty's companies forming the second. Clark was ahead of them all.

Their goal, beyond the watery plain, was high ground above Vincennes, lying north along the Wabash. There were obvious reasons for moving after nightfall, though the direction of their movement—chiefly through waist-deep water—was cut off from view from the fort by the terrain. One of the reasons set down by Clark was to give no one "oppertunity of seeing our Troops before dark," lest the French lose heart at the limited numbers of men behind Clark.

At or about eight o'clock that evening they reached the high
ground above the town. This ground was not actually sizable
enough to be called a "hill"; it was more a ridge-like knoll or
mound, but it effectively commanded the settlement. From the
high ground, Clark and his men began to move quietly into Vincennes, seizing the main street without encountering even token
opposition. Clark stationed some of his men, and the rest of them
were drawn to the houses of the French residents. The doors stood
open, the tables were heaped high with food and the men fell to it.

The French inhabitants assured Clark that Fort Sackville had
just been repaired. Indeed, the repairs had been completed only
"that eavening," as Hamilton had ordered, but hasty reconnoiter-
ing showed that there were major openings in the palisades of
such a nature that anyone standing behind them would not be
safe from gunfire. Nevertheless, Fort Sackville presented a formidable appearance, and Clark was not disposed to underrate the
defense Hamilton might be able to put up. Nor was he inclined
to be any less bold in his approach to it.

He sent Lieutenant Bayley to attack the fort on signal. He
sent out another patrol to intercept two British soldiers who had
been dispatched to search for the army Hamilton had been informed was somewhere about. One of them was the same Francis
Maisonville who had first informed Hamilton of Clark's capture
of Kaskaskia and Cahokia. Bayley and his fourteen men were
instructed to begin firing on Fort Sackville and to continue fire
until relieved by another force.

Yet it was three hours before any shots were fired. The men
with Bayley were seasoned woodsmen. They approached the fort
and took good cover without being challenged by any sentry.
Indeed, there was no evidence that anyone in the fort saw anything unusual in their deployment before the main gate, though
this complacency was hardly surprising, for there was nothing to
distinguish Clark's men from the French Canadians in Vincennes,
particularly in the darkness. At that hour, too, the moon was soon
to set.

Fort Sackville was not entirely unprepared. Having heard from
scouts reports of an enemy force in the vicinity, Hamilton had

issued ammunition for the blockhouses and had put up scaffolding for small-arms fire in the north and south angles of the fort, so that men could fire over the palisades instead of through the loopholes. He had recalled absent soldiers, had alerted the Vincennes militia and had had additional rations of corn and rum brought into the fort.

When the firing began, Governor Hamilton was at a game of cards with his prisoner, Lieutenant Helm. Such firing was not necessarily a portent of danger. Indians occasionally fired off their guns. So did the French. A few more shots were heard. But it was not until a volley was fired that Hamilton left his card game and had his men stand to arms. Even then, he did not entertain the thought that the fort was under attack. Finally one of his sergeants was hit by a glancing bullet. Only then did Hamilton order his men to man the blockhouses and firing platforms. The matrosses manned the guns but looked in vain for a target. Even then, however, Hamilton was at a loss to understand the attack on the fort. Clark and his men from the Illinois country were the last attackers he could think of, what with all the inundated land between Kaskaskia and Vincennes.

He was not long in doubt, however. His surgeon McBeath, who had been in the village when the firing started, managed to make his way back into Fort Sackville with an account crediting Clark with five hundred men under arms. As the firing was increasing and the attack on Fort Sackville was soon being mounted from three sides, Hamilton found it easy to believe his surgeon's information. The fort's defenders began to return the fire pouring into Fort Sackville.

Meanwhile, outside the fort, Clark's forces were augmented:

> The Kickepous and Peankeshaws to the amount of about one hundred, that was in Town immediately Armed themselves in our favour and Marched to attack the Fort. I thanked the Chief for his intended service, told him the Ill consequence of our People being mingled in the dark, that they might lay in their quarters until light, he Approved of it and sent off his Troops, appeared to be much elivated himself and staid with me giving all the Information he could.

The artillery from Fort Sackville did no damage. The fort was now entirely surrounded, and heavy fire was steady from both sides. Clark was confident of victory:

In a few hours I found my Prize sure, Certain of taking every Man that I could have wished for, being the whole of those that incited the Indians to War: all my past sufferings vanished: never was a Man more happy. It wanted no encouragement from any Officer to inflame our Troops with a Martial Spirit. The knowledge of the Person they attacked and the thoughts of their massacred friends was Sufficient.[21]

Clark's men found cover behind picket fences, barns, houses and the nearby church, though Hamilton's artillery fire made the church and the churchyard fence uncomfortable. Hamilton's fire power was not inefficient, but he had no idea of how many men encircled the fort; and, as throughout the attack Clark continued his stage tactics designed to make the besieged British believe that there was a greater army outside than in fact he had, Hamilton concluded that the attacking force was a very large one, capable of supplying new detachments of troops every little while.

Some of the French from Vincennes joined Clark's men with their own weapons. They had previously supplied Clark with the dry powder he needed, for, what with rain and constant wading through deep water, little dry powder was to be had among the men from Kaskaskia. There was ample powder and weaponry within Fort Sackville, but the position of the defenders was precarious because of the poorly constructed palisade. Clark's men were sharpshooters each of whom could put a bullet through the smallest opening.

From the fort, Hamilton could see some obvious preparation for the construction of a trench under the eleven-foot palisade. He trained artillery on the activity, not knowing whether it was bluff or not. Clark, meanwhile, was waiting for Captain Rogers and the *Willing*, which was bringing his own artillery. Then he could, with a well-placed shot, blow up the powder magazine and the fort. But there was no sign of the *Willing*.

Hamilton ordered as many openings in the palisade as possible covered, but it was impossible to close them all, and there was

deadly danger in going too close to them for any purpose whatever. Four of the British were wounded and taken to the officers'
quarters. Clark's men managed to silence two of the fort's guns,
wounding the matrosses through the gun ports. Hamilton finally
had to order the gun ports closed, for each open port invited
such a volley of fire that the risk of losing men outweighed any
advantage the artillery might have given the defenders. The
British guns were bolted to timber carriages on wheels. Each time
a gun was fired, the piece had to be drawn back inside the fort
and the gun port shuttered. When the gun was ready to fire
again, it had to be wheeled back and its muzzle thrust through
the gun port and put into position to fire, not by means of any
mechanical devices but by men sighting along the barrel; they
made easy targets for the sharpshooting Virginians.

The attack upon the fort continued throughout the night.
Sometimes the firing was heavy, sometimes sporadic. Sometimes
there was a lull following heavy firing, then another round of
heavy firing, which the besieged Hamilton took for proof that
fresh troops were constantly replacing those in the line—a conclusion Clark hoped for when he ordered this theatrical tactic. Clark
saw to it, too, that there was much hearty laughter in the background, as if to convey the men's assurance that their numbers
were so great that the fort must fall no matter what measures
Hamilton might take.

Apprised that La Mothe and Maisonville and their party had
effected a return to Vincennes and were concealed not far from
Fort Sackville hoping for a chance to slip into the fort, Clark
deliberately made an opening through which La Mothe and his
men—without Maisonville, who had been betrayed to the Virginians by a relative in Vincennes—could rush the fort and climb
over the palisades. Clark reasoned soundly that he would far
sooner have La Mothe and his party under fire in the fort than
free to go and rouse Indians friendly to the British and bring them
down upon the Virginians' rear. Maisonville was a prize, for his
activities on behalf of the British were widely known; Clark
spared him all but a piece of his scalp and sent him behind the
lines as a prisoner.

The night wore away. In midmorning Clark called a halt to the firing and sent a man under the flag with a letter to Hamilton:

> Sir In order to save yourself from the Impending Storm that now Threatens you I order you to Immediately surrender yourself up with all your Garrison Stores &c, &c. for if I am obliged to storm, you may depend upon such Treatment justly due to a Murderer beward of destroying Stores of any kind or any papers or letters that is in your possession or hurting one house in the Town for by heavens if you do there shall be no Mercy shewn you.

Hamilton was not impressed by Clark's letter. Although Clark might have artillery hidden somewhere, there was nothing in sight to justify his implied threat to storm Fort Sackville. Furthermore, the wording and general phraseology of Clark's letter only underscored Hamilton's opinion of the wild, unlettered Virginians. He sent his cold reply:

"Govr Hamilton begs leave to acquaint Col. Clark that he and his Garrison are not disposed to be awed into any action Unworthy of British subjects." He had read both letters before his garrison: "The English men all declared their resolution of defending the King's colors to the last man, rather than abide the mercy of the Rebels." [22]

He could not say as much of the French. Indeed, the Frenchmen within the fort, for all that they were manifestly on the British side, had grave reservations about firing upon the attackers, for it was clear in the light of the morning that many of their own people had armed themselves and were fighting with the Americans. At that point, Hamilton knew privately that he must "accept honorable terms if they could be obtained."

The firing began once more. It was "very hot on both sides," as Captain Bowman observed, though "None of our men wounded; several of the men in the Fort wounded through the port holes." This renewed firing and the uncertainty about the dependability of the Frenchmen inside Fort Sackville persuaded Hamilton to make another try for a cessation of hostilities. This time he sent out Lieutenant Helm under the flag. Helm came out smartly and presented Hamilton's letter to Clark:

Govr. Hamilton proposed to Col. Clark a truce for three days; during which time he proposes there shall be no defensive work carried on in the garrison, on condition that Col. Clark shall observe, on his part, a like cessation of any offensive work. That is, he wishes to confer with Col. Clark as soon as can be; and promises, that whatever may pass between them two and another person mutually agreed upon to be present, shall remain secret till matters be finished, as he wishes that whatever the result of their conference, it may be to the honour and credit of each party. If Col. Clark makes a difficulty of coming into the fort, Lieut. Gov. Hamilton will speak to him by the gate.[23]

This proposal was patently absurd. Perhaps Hamilton hoped to gain time for the arrival of the British party that Clark knew to be somewhere north of Vincennes. It was not a proposal that Clark could entertain for an instant. He sent Helm back with a curt refusal but made a counterproposal, suggesting that if the Governor wanted a conference Clark would meet him at the nearby church, which virtually abutted the property on which Fort Sackville stood.

At that point in the negotiations a diversion occurred. A party of Indians friendly to the British came into Vincennes and approached the fort. Clark expected them, for some of the friendly Kickapoo had warned him prior to their actual appearance. Captain John Williams rode out openly to meet them, very probably counting on the Indians' mistaking him and his little company of men for inhabitants of Vincennes. As a result, the Indian war party, some members of which carried fresh scalps, and two French prisoners with them were taken by Clark's men.

"The Poor Devils never discovered their mistake until it was too late for many of them to escape." But this sentence was the only expression of sympathy that Clark permitted himself. He saw in these prisoners an ideal opportunity to impress the Indians with the poor protection that the British offered them. There was not, in any event, much Clark could do to spare their lives, for it was precisely this kind of raiding party that had time and again descended upon the settlements of Kentucky, killing and scalping men, women and children. And again, it was a party sent out by Hamilton, who had a notorious if somewhat unjustified reputa-

tion for inciting the Indians to pillage and kill, although this party
was essentially for scouting. The Indians had indulged their lust
for scalps on the side.

Some of the Indians, though wounded, escaped. The French
prisoners were immediately freed. Nine Indians were securely
pinioned. Captain McCarty intervened for one of the Indians,
whom he recognized as the son of the Ottawa Chief Pontiac, who
had once saved McCarty's life. Clark spared the Chief's son. One
of the white men with the party, though painted like the Indians,
turned out to be the son of one of Clark's lieutenants. His life,
too, was spared. But the remaining Indians were ordered to sit in
a circle in plain sight of the fort; knowing what was coming, they
began to sing the death chant.

Thereupon the Indians were tomahawked in sight of the defenders of Fort Sackville. Hamilton was horrified at the butchery,
without reflecting that even worse scenes, involving women and
children, had been enacted out of his sight at the hands of Indians sent out from Detroit by him; if Clark was guilty in this
instance of "butchery," as Hamilton put it in his report, so had
Hamilton been, on more than one occasion. Clark counted on the
dispatching of the Indians to have a salubrious effect on the garrison behind the palisades of Fort Sackville.

"After such a scene," concluded Hamilton, "we had little hope
of being very secure in a capitulation." Nevertheless, Clark had
to be dealt with—and increasingly on his own terms. Hamilton
took counsel with Major Jehu Hay about the chance of escaping
by night down the Wabash, unaware that the *Willing* was not
far down river and would have prevented their escape, but this
plan was quickly abandoned, for the garrison wounded could
hardly be taken along.

Without further delay, Hamilton went out to meet Clark at the
church. He took Lieutenant Helm along. There was much indeci-
sive talk between them. All firing, of course, had ceased. Clark
maintained that the British position was hopeless. Hamilton dis-
agreed. Clark bluntly counted off the number of men on whom
Hamilton could depend—fewer than forty. He pointed out also
that his own artillery would be in position in a few hours' time—

before that February 24 wore away—and, if the fort had to be stormed, no man in it would be saved.

Both men grew heated, Clark by the memory of the many Indian raids and their savagery and Hamilton by Clark's insistence on what he took to be humiliating terms. Lieutenant Helm did his best to persuade both men to control their tempers. Two or three times the men parted, standing aside and ready to give over talk and resume the battle.

At last Hamilton decried the desire of the Americans to fight rather than retreat an inch from their unreasonable demands. Having pushed the British commander this far, Clark offered to send a list of conditions for the surrender of Fort Sackville; this offer was a retreat from the demand to surrender "at discretion," and Hamilton accepted it.

Both men returned to their posts to discuss matters with their officers. Clark found his own officers ready to modify the conditions of surrender. Accordingly, he sent into the fort a list of terms, as those Hamilton had offered were not satisfactory.

Hamilton was to deliver up Fort Sackville as it stood—it had not suffered much in the battle and could readily be repaired and improved over the condition in which the British repairs had left it—with all stores and supplies of whatever nature it contained. The garrison must march out at ten o'clock the following morning as prisoners of war, with all its arms and belongings. The garrison would be allowed three days to settle accounts with the inhabitants and traders of Vincennes. The officers of the garrison would be allowed the necessary baggage.

Nothing was said of dignity and safe conduct, but so much had been promised by Clark at the outset, however much, he had said, it went against his grain to overlook the inciting of the Indians against the helpless American settlements. These terms were not much better than unconditional surrender, but they saved a little of Hamilton's face.

He signed. But he could not forbear appending a paragraph between the date, "at Post St. Vincents, 24th Feb., 1779," and his signature, "Henry Hamilton, Lieut. Gov. and Superintendent": "Agreed to for the following reasons: The remoteness from succors; the state and quantity of provisions, &c.; unanimity of officers and men in its expediency; the honourable terms allowed; and, lastly, the confidence in a generous enemy."

The formal surrender took place the next morning. While two companies of Clark's men stood on parade outside the fort flanking the gate, Hamilton's troops marched out and surrendered their arms. Clark and some of his men marched in. There was no need to strike the British flag, for, after it had been hauled down the night before, Hamilton had spared himself and his men the humiliation of raising it in the morning.

Once inside, Clark's men wanted to salute the thirteen United States with the six-pounder, though all the gunners who knew how to handle artillery were on the *Willing*, which had still not reached Vincennes, though it was not far away. The men bungled and managed to blow up a cask of six-pounder cartridges placed too near, which, despite all the damage it did, made a satisfyingly resounding explosion audible for miles around Vincennes.

Clark renamed the fort "Patrick Henry" after the Governor of Virginia and raised the American flag.

III

The Long Knives Against the Indians

If there had been no George Rogers Clark, a vast expanse of America today would, almost certainly, have been something different from what it is—probably British, just possibly Spanish. The sturdy, adventurous youngster, with the sandy red hair, keenly interested in wild lands and wilder nature, and—wildest of all—the red man, had barely reached maturity when a brave new world opened suddenly for just such youths as he. Gaily and gallantly he went to it. Brilliantly, he conquered it. . . . By his middle twenties, George Rogers Clark had saved the "back country" for America. From the Mississippi frontier he had established, the new frontier went on, westward. By his middle twenties, he had made a national reputation, won the admiration of Washington, become the dominant figure of that new West which he had made his own, and his country's.

—John Bakeless,
Background to Glory

1

Clark settled in at the fort, and repairs went forward. For the time being, Hamilton and his officers remained prisoners, but Clark was sensible of the fact that Hamilton was too great a prize to be kept at the fort, lest a superior British force be tempted to take him back. Clark knew very well that he himself, Father Gibault, perhaps Francis Vigo and some of the defecting Frenchmen were high on the list of wanted men in Detroit.

The very first matter to be attended to was that of the British supplies waiting at the Maumee to come down the Wabash and restock the fort. No time must be lost, for as soon as the British commander at Detroit, Captain Lernoult, learned of the loss of Vincennes, he was certain to send for the supplies, turning them back from the post along the lower Wabash. While Hamilton was trying in vain to induce Clark to change sides, though he held the American soldiers in contempt as bandits, Helm—now promoted by Clark to captain—together with a force of men, was moving up the Wabash to the Maumee.

Hamilton was still at Fort Patrick Henry when Helm returned. The Captain had captured the British supply boats and everything they held—arms, ammunition, liquor, clothing. The Americans fell upon the booty; hundreds of shirts and uniforms were distributed among Clark's men, and the wine and brandy went down throats unaccustomed to such fare. There were six tons of supplies, worth conservatively $50,000, the legitimate spoils of war.

His prisoners were Clark's next concern. Guarding them taxed his own men. He resolved upon another bold stroke, which wore the guise of generosity. He chose from among the prisoners the French militia from Detroit, called it together and made a speech in which he promised a return to Detroit without delay. Indeed, the French were to keep the boats that took them back up the Wabash and sell them, if they liked, at Detroit. He gave them a copy of the treaty of alliance between France and the Americans, his intention being to have it circulated among the French at Detroit and to spread disaffection there.

Furthermore, he sent a challenging letter to Captain Richard Lernoult, who was in command at Detroit: "I learn by your letter to Govr. Hamilton that you were very busy making new works, I am glad to hear it, as it saves the Ammericans some expences in building." In it, he clearly announced his intention to attack Detroit as soon as feasible. Indeed, Detroit as the ultimate goal of his entire Illinois campaign was never much out of Clark's thoughts, though he realized that he could not take that post without a considerably augmented force and specific orders from the Governor of Virginia. The letter to which Clark referred had been among various communications in the baggage taken at Maumee. The raid on the Maumee had also added to the prisoners: 38 privates, most of whom went back to Detroit forthwith, and two more important personages: the Grand Judge of Detroit, Philip Dejean, and a commissary, neither of whom was detained for long at Fort Patrick Henry, for Clark was in haste to move his British prisoners out of reach of any possible conflict.

Clark's next order of business was the disposal of Governor Hamilton. For all Hamilton's instructions to his Indian allies to be humane in their conquests, he must certainly have known that they were savages, most of them, inured to cruelty and incapable of humanity as Hamilton understood it, given not only to scalping but also to burning selected victims at the stake. Clark knew that the government of Virginia would look upon Hamilton as a desirable prisoner, and he lost no time in dispatching him, together with Major Jehu Hay and other officers, to Williamsburg.

They set out, according to Major Bowman's journal, on March 7, in the charge of Captain John Williams, whose task it was to see the party of 27 prisoners guarded by 23 Americans as far as the Falls of the Ohio, and Lieutenant John Rogers, who would be in command from the Falls to Williamsburg. Hamilton, who expected to be treated as befitted an officer, was to be sadly disillusioned, for he had to go partly on foot through the Kentucky country where his very name, because of the Indian raids on the settlements, was loathed. He was in imminent danger of being seized and slain for what his Indians had done—the same things he was so outraged at seeing Clark's men do to his Indians before Fort Sackville—and, far from being received as befitted his station, he was promptly ordered into irons and a jail cell by Governor Thomas Jefferson, who had succeeded Patrick Henry, once the party reached Williamsburg.

With Hamilton and the officers off his hands, Clark turned his attention to the Indians.

> I knew that Mr. Hamilton had endeavoured to make them believe that we intended at last to take all their Lands from them, and that in case of Success, we would shew no greater Mercy for those who did not Join him than those that did, I indeavoured to make myself acquainted with the Arguments he used; And calling together the neighbouring Nations, Peankeshaws, Kicke-

poes, & others that would not listen to him Indeavored to un-
deceive them. I made a very long Speach to them in the Indian
manner, Extoll'd them to the Skies for their Manly behaviour and
fedility; told them that we were so far from having any design
on their Lands, that I looked upon it that we were then on their
Land where the Fort stood, that we claimed no Land in their
Country; that the first Man that offered to take their Lands by
Violence must strike the tomhk in my head; that it was only necessary that I should be in their Country during the War and
keep a Fort in it to drive off the English, who had a design
against all People; after that I might go to some place where I
could get Land to support Me ... they were much pleased at
what they heard, and begged me to favour them the next day
with my Compy at a Council of theirs. I accordingly Attended;
greatest part of the time spent in Ceremony, they at last told me
that they had been meditating on what I had said the day before:
that all the Nations would be rejoiced to have me always in their
Country as their great Father and Protector. . . .[1]

But these Indians had shown the Americans and the French
friendship before. There were others who had not. The Shawnee
still raided the Kentucky settlements; there were Indian villages
in the Illinois countries friendly to the British. Clark wasted little
time or sympathy on them. There were no councils or speeches.
He sent out detachments to show force and cow them into
submission.

It was time, too, for Clark to return to Kaskaskia, where Fort
Clark was now under the direction of Captain Robert George,
who had come up from New Orleans with a force of 41 men; he
had taken the place of the commander Clark had left, one Jas.
Willings, who had resigned and gone back to Philadelphia.

On March 20 Clark was ready to depart. This time, however,
there would be no forced march through water and mud. His
men left Vincennes by boat, accompanied by the *Willing*, which
had finally reached Vincennes after the fort had been captured;
it was placed under the command of Captain McCarty. There
were five sizable boats and one lesser craft oddly called *Running
Fly*. They set out in the late afternoon.

Lieutenant Richard Brashears was left in command at Fort
Patrick Henry. His fellow officers were Lieutenant John Bailey

and Lieutenant Abraham Chapline. They had forty men. Captain Leonard Helm was put in command of Vincennes itself, Moses Henry was left as Indian agent and Patrick Kennedy was installed as quartermaster. They were empowered to deal with the Indians or to send them to Kaskaskia, for, as an aftermath of Clark's generosity with the Indians on the one hand and his bold courage on the other—both qualities the Indians admired—Indian chiefs from many tribes came into Vincennes to treat for peace and friendship and, of course, gifts, if they could be obtained. For, if the Indians renounced the British, they expected to be paid for it.

Clark, busy with plans for an advance on Detroit, found that he had to concern himself also with finances and supplies. Though he was formally thanked for his work in bringing the western portions of Virginia into the union of states by both the Virginia Assembly and the Continental Congress, those bodies were no better informed about the cost of maintaining the peace and pacifying the Indians than either the French or British governments had been before them.

Clark had reason to expect more men. He had sent for five hundred, and they had been promised to him. People were coming into Kentucky in increasing numbers, having gained confidence from the news of Clark's victories in Illinois. But the men eluded him; Colonel John Montgomery, sent to recruit them, came back with only 150, who arrived well after the date Clark had set. And he had reason for urgency, for all his intelligence from Detroit was to the effect that the defenses of that post, as well as those of Fort Michilimackinac in the straits between Lakes Huron and Michigan, were demoralized and that their commanders—Captain Richard Berringer Lernoult at Detroit and Major Arent S. De Peyster at Michilimackinac—were fearful of being taken by Clark and his Big Knives. The situation brooked little delay, for to the south the British post of Natchez still had to be taken.

But it was not only the men that did not come. There was little food, arms, ammunition, clothing, and many of Clark's men at Vincennes had been literally in rags, which were replaced only by the British clothing seized at the Maumee. Money was even more of a problem, for, though Virginia kept Clark supplied with currency, that currency was rapidly losing its value, as the British were counterfeiting it with some success. Congress finally issued new currency, ordering the old bills to be turned in by a certain date; it was not until that date had long passed that the frontier learned of it. The French merchants with whom Clark dealt found themselves in possession of worthless money.

Clark was forced to operate largely on credit. He ordered what he needed and in payment wrote drafts on Oliver Pollock, a well-known merchant who had conducted a business in Louisiana for twenty years. He was established in New Orleans and had been appointed commercial agent for the United States in mid-1777. He was authorized to supply Clark directly if possible and to honor his drafts. Congress—or Virginia—would honor Pollock's drafts in turn, but with the decline in value of the American currency such funds as were sent to Pollock were unacceptable to the merchants of New Orleans. A proposal to send Pollock flour to be used in bartering for supplies, though sound enough, failed for lack of flour. Nor could he get furs, bear oil, flour or anything else from Clark and the French in Illinois.

Yet Pollock managed to supply Clark sufficiently to keep his men in reasonably good shape. He sent munitions bought from Spanish agents, large amounts of gunpowder and even, on occasion, swivel guns—the kind of light artillery that was especially useful in wilderness country. Pollock was not alone in helping Clark. Francis Vigo and another merchant whom Clark had first taken, then set free in Kaskaskia, Gabriel Cerré, did their utmost for the American cause. All three men seriously impaired their own fortunes by trying to assist Clark; Pollock went so far as to draw upon his own resources, selling and mortgaging property to keep Clark in control in the Illinois country.

At last Clark took a disastrous step as far as his personal fortunes were concerned; in order to have his drafts honored, he sold and mortgaged his own property, personally guaranteeing payment of such drafts as were presented. He impoverished himself, but he kept his army mobile and functional, and, most important, he saved the Illinois country and the old Northwest Territory for the United States.

Yet he lacked the men he needed even to take the most obvious and elementary measures. He did not need Pollock's urging to recognize that the British posts along the Mississippi south of the Ohio ought to be taken; Pollock constantly held up the threat of Spanish seizure. He knew whereof he wrote to Clark. In September 1779, just over half a year after Clark's brilliant seizure of Vincennes, Governor Bernardo de Gálvez moved up from New Orleans to attack the posts and seize them for Spain. They were thus beyond Clark's reach, for, with the British looming on the north, he could not afford to antagonize the Spanish to the south and west, though he had full information from Pollock and others in regard to the British posts—how many troops manned them, how well they were fortified, what gunpower was to be expected and the dedication or lack of it among the troops.

By that time Clark was no longer at Kaskaskia. He had gone to the Falls of the Ohio, for he had concluded—unwittingly reviving the dream of Governor Jean Baptiste le Moyne de Bienville—that a fort must be built at or near the mouth of the Ohio to prevent the movement of British and Indians to the Mississippi and the possible depredations of the Spanish from the other direction. He had made careful representations to Governor Patrick Henry for the construction of such a fort as part of his grand plan, which still included an attack on Detroit and elimination of the British from the Great Lakes country south of Mackinac.

Meanwhile, on September 4 Thomas Jefferson replaced Patrick Henry as Governor of Virginia. On that same day, ironically, the General Assembly voted to bestow on Clark "an elegant Sword" in recognition of "Col. Clarkes important services in the reduction of Fort St. Vincents." The sword was something neither he nor his men could eat, and, upon its presentation together with a protest about one of his drafts, the angry Clark thrust the blade into the ground, broke it and kicked the hilt into the Ohio, after which he returned word to the Governor that such insignias were useless to him "while they refused his starving soldiers the common necessaries of life." [2]

Word presently reached Clark of Jefferson's approval of his plan for a fort at the mouth of the Ohio. On September 23, 1779, Clark wrote Governor Jefferson:

I am happy to find that your Sentiments Respecting a fortification at or near the Mouth of Ohio is so agreable to the Ideas of Every Man of any Judgment in this Department it is the Spot that ought to be strongly Fortified and all other garisons in the Western Cuntrey depend on it if the Ground would admit of it but the Misfortune is their is not a Acre of Ground near the point than four Miles up the Ohio but what is often Ten Feet under Water About twelve Miles below the point their is a beautiful Situation as if by nature designed for a fortification (by every observation that has been taken lays a Quarter of a degree within the State of Virginia) its Ellevation is such that a small Expence would Render it very Strong and of greater advantage than one four Miles up the Ohio in Case you have one built a few years will prove the Propriety of it it would Amediately become the key of the whole Trade of the Western Cuntrey and well Situated for the Indian department in General Besides Many Salutary effects it would Rendr during the War by Awing our Enemies the Chicasaws and the English posts on the Mississipie the Strength of the Garison ought not to be less than two Hundred men after built, A Hundred Families that might Easily be got to Settle in a Town would be of great advantage in promoting the place I am Sensible that the Spaniards would be fond to Settle a post of Correspondence opposite to it if the Ground would admit but the Cuntrey on their Side is so Subject to Inundation that its Impossible—for the want of Such a post I find it absolutely nessesary to Station an armed Boat at the Point So as to Command the Navigation of Both Rivers to defend our Trading Boats and Stop the great Concourse of Toryes and deserters that pass down the River to our Enemies.

The Illinois under its present Circumstances, is by no means able to Supply the Troops that you Expect in this department with provitions as the Crops at St. Vincines was so Exceedingly bad that upwards of Five Hundred Souls will have to depend on their neighbours for Bread I Should be exceedingly glad that you would Commission Some person to furnish the Troops in this Quarter with provitions as the greatest part must Come from the Frontiers for the Ensuing year as I cant depend on the Illinois for Greater Supplys than will be Suffitient for two Hundred and fifty Men. . . .

He added a postscript on his disappointment about an intended excursion up the Wabash to attack the British.[3]

Typically, without waiting for a reply or formal orders to construct a fort near the mouth of the Ohio, he wrote a week later to Captain Silas Martin, Commander of the Militia:

> Whareas a Fort is Intended amediately to be Built near the Mouth of the Ohio and a number of artifitiers wanting to Carry on the Works as well as other Inhabitants
>
> I do by the Virtue of the power and authority to me Given Authorize you to Raise any number of Persons that you Can get to become Settlers at Said Post the whole to be under pay as Melitia as long as Nessessary you are to Rendezvous, at this place by the First Day of December next.[4]

Orders were dispatched with enthusiasm, but the men were lacking to carry them out readily. Conditions that autumn were difficult, and the winter looming ahead looked grim. On October 10 Captain James Shelby, then in command at Fort Patrick Henry, which he was still calling "Post St. Vinston," wrote to his commander that he had received from Kaskaskia:

> no Sepplys of Provisions Sence your departure which Renders Much Confution having no Salt have Rendored at leest Two thirds of the men incapbile of duty, the Gentlemen of this Villege have Continued fornishing Beef but now Say it is out of their Power to furnish aney more. We are in an Exceeding Bad Condition at Present & am afeard that Nesessity will oblig avacuation of this Post with out sum Speedy Releif Sence I Returned from Ouia have sent Two Differint Expresses to Colo. Montgumry and have not yet Recd an answer. I can Send no huntars out for meet by Reeson of haveing no salt I hope when you are Bettor Informed of our Condition by the Gentlemen now Going to the falls which I refer you to for Pirticalars that you will be kind enough to Send me amediate derections in what Mannor I am to act for which I Shall Wate with the Greatest Impatiant....[5]

While Captain John Rogers waited in Williamsburg for an order to raise troops, as provided by a recent act of Assembly, and to petition the Assembly to repair its omissions in regard to the men in the Illinois country, Clark called a council of war on November 16, 1779. Captains Robert George, Thomas Quirk, Edward Worthington, Richard Harrison and John Bailey were present to consider the questions Colonel Clark thought urgent: How many troops were necessary to reduce Detroit or the "Floridians" on the Mississippi? How to provision them? If they were to be provisioned from the Illinois, what would it require annually? What fortifications were vital to the Illinois country? How much could be counted on from the inhabitants of the Illinois country for provisions?

The officers did their best to be realistic about the proposal to reduce Detroit:

> ... Considering the present state of Detroit, and the well-affected dispositions of the adjacent inhabitants, do conceive that that post might be reduced by a few well-disciplined troops, but as these troops have a long, tedious and fatiguing march all the way through a hostile country, exposed to frequent interruptions and attacks from the savages, our natural enemy, as well as many unforeseen accidents, consequently attendant on long marches, they are unanimously of opinion that not less than one thousand troops would be requisite for effecting that purpose. . . .

In view of the difficulty of recruiting men for the western country, the officers could as well have asked for ten times that number.

Clark was not unmindful of the Spanish posts on the west bank of the Mississippi, particularly since relations between Spain and Great Britain had now reached a point at which war between them had been declared, and an expedition against the Spanish posts had actually been ordered by the British command in Quebec. If it became necessary to prevent the taking of the Spanish posts by the British, Clark was confident that 500 men under his command could seize the posts before the British got there, very likely counting on a preference for the Americans among the Spanish, as well as on the openly-expressed Spanish sympathy for the American cause over that of the British.

Provisions, however, remained the most nettlesome problem. The officers were not optimistic on this score, in view of the straitened circumstances in which the men and the inhabitants alike now lived. "Supplies of bread kind can be furnished from the Illinois country, but as to the meat species, it must come from some part of the Ohio or waters east thereof." The troops, in short, could not be expected to draw their substance from the Illinois country.

The officers were also of the opinion that the three forts then standing in the Illinois country plus the proposed fort were sufficient:

> ... One at Kahokia, one at Post St. Vincent, one at Auabache, and one at or near the mouth of the Ohio, in the most convenient place on the banks of the Mississippi, each fortification to be one hundred feet square in the clear within the walls, to be built of earth dug out of an entrenchment ten feet deep, with earth thrown upon the inside of said entrenchment, must form a wall of ten feet high and eight feet thick, which with the entrenchment, which will form a wall of twenty feet perpendicular, on the top of which they conceive it necessary there should be a wooden wall of sawed or hewn timber ten feet high, twelve inches thick, with bastions at each corner so proportioned that one shall clear another. The garrison at Kahokia to consist of one hundred and fifty troops, and the garrison at Post St. Vincent of one hundred and fifty troops, and the garrison at or near the mouth of Ohio, two hundred troops.[6]

Late in January 1780, Jefferson's instructions to Clark came from Williamsburg. Not only was Clark authorized to construct a fort on suitable ground near the mouth of the Ohio, but he was also told to

> take such care of the men under you as an economical householder would of his own family doing everything within himself as far as he can & calling for as few supplies as possible, the less you depend for supplies from this Quarter the less you will be disappointed by those impediments distance & a precarious foreign Commerce.

Jefferson suggested that Clark ought "to withdraw as many of your men as you can from the West side of the Ohio, leaving only so many as may be necessary for keeping the Illinois Settlements in Spirits & for their real defence." There was much more in Jefferson's long letter: a promise of a "Troop of Horse" coming with

Captain John Rogers but only a promise that a request for a second would be laid before the Assembly. There were references to "the distress of the Public Treasury." [7]

Jefferson was cognizant of the fact that matters were about to grow much more difficult, for the British, late in 1778, had begun to turn south and had taken Savannah. Throughout 1779, the Americans had suffered the loss of many men in the South. Furthermore, the Spanish entry into the war had not disturbed the status quo in North America, for Spain had neither recognized the United States nor pressed its war with England on the Continent. The year closed with a disastrous assault on Savannah, in the course of which the Americans, with French help, lost almost a thousand men; the British were preparing to attack Charleston, which fell to them in the spring of 1780.

If Clark was aware of what was going on far east of his position, he left no evidence of it in his letters. While the British were besieging Charleston, Clark was being petitioned to do something to save Kentucky from continuous harassment by the Shawnee. The inhabitants of Boonesborough wrote him on March 10, begging him to help them:

> The few among us who have long experienced the intolerable hardships of maintaining our Post against the Barbarous savages, Derive very little consolation from the vast addition of Numbers now scattered through the various Parts of this Country. The almost incredible number of Distressed and defenceless Families settled through our woods for the sake of sustinance instead of adding to our strength are in fact, so many allurements, and must become a daily sacrifice to the savage brutality of our inhuman enemies. . . . In this Critical and alarming situation we beg leave to implore your Assistance—We are fully persuaded that nothing less than a Vigorous expedition against the Shawnee Towns will Put an end to their Depradations, or secure the Peace and safety of these Settlements. [8]

On March 13, inhabitants of Bryan's Station sent him a similar petition, promising to send men to join Clark in a raid on the Shawnee towns. Clark was upset by the petitions and responsive to them. He wrote to Colonel William Fleming at Harrodsburg on

April 4 that he was "hartily sorry for the great loss of Blood and property Sustained by the Kentuckians." In the meantime, the citizens of Cahokia were also asking help, for Indians—doubtless spurred on by the British from Detroit—so menaced them that they could not cultivate their fields. Such intelligence as reached Clark from the north suggested that the British were organizing a concerted effort on the part of the Indians; the government at Quebec was apparently hoping to seize control of all the Mississippi Valley, including New Orleans, and counting on the British force in Florida under General John Campbell to cross to New Orleans, seize it and move up the Mississippi to join forces with men coming down from Detroit.

The inhabitants of Cahokia sent their message to Clark by Charles Gratiot, who also carried an appeal from Governor Leyba at St. Louis, whose information was similar to that of the citizens of Cahokia. Clark reacted immediately. As Fort Jefferson had been built as planned, its construction no longer solely occupied him; gathering together as many men as he could, he set out for St. Louis, a hundred miles up the Mississippi. He went directly to St. Louis to confer with Leyba, who was ailing and had little heart for battle, for his own death impended; the Spanish Governor proposed that Clark head the defense of St. Louis, but Clark's first obligation was to Cahokia. The Indian force sent by the British was in any event still a day away.

After this conference, Clark crossed to Cahokia and there concealed his troops to await the arrival of the Indians, who, when at last they came, were easily defeated and routed. Their subsequent attack on St. Louis failed, in part at least because word passed among them that Clark was in the city and they lost heart at this misinformation and withdrew. Clark, however, was of no mind to let matters rest at that point; he dispatched Colonel John Montgomery to follow and harass them. Montgomery chased them all the way to Peoria, burned a few Indian villages and withdrew, thereby helping materially to ruin the British plans for control of the Mississippi.

Clark himself had more urgent matters to attend to. The actions at Cahokia and St. Louis had resulted in the taking of prisoners and deserters. They gave accounts of a major force, under

Captain Henry Bird, that was on its way from Detroit to capture
Fort Nelson at the Falls of the Ohio and meant to invade and
conquer Kentucky. Clark hastened back to Fort Jefferson.

As he moved up the Ohio, he had to pass through a narrow
part of the river between an island and the shore. His alertness
possibly saved his life, for he caught sight of strange Indians in
war paint on both sides of the waterway, lurking in ambush. Instantly he sprang to his feet and began to signal elaborately, as
to an army following him. The Indians, more fearful of an army
they could not see than of one they could, hesitated and finally
drew back, so that Clark reached Fort Jefferson in safety.

Captain Bird and his force were not far away, preparing to
attack Fort Nelson at the Falls, when word of Clark's presence
spread among the Indians, who were superstitiously afraid of the
redheaded leader of the Big Knives. Rumor had it that Clark had
hastened from Fort Jefferson to Fort Nelson and was waiting for
the attack. Much to Bird's dismay, confident as he was that he
had the superior force and that his field guns—a six-pounder and a
three-pounder—could reduce Fort Nelson, the Indians decided to
hold a council.

The council went on for two days. Many of the chiefs made
speeches, the gist of which was that it would be dangerous to
attack Fort Nelson with the chief of the Big Knives there. It
would be better to attack the weakly fortified lesser settlements
like Ruddle's Station and Martin's Station, both on Licking River.

And there they went. Both Ruddle's and Martin's Stations fell
to Bird's artillery. It might have been possible to penetrate farther
into Kentucky, but by that time Bird had already taken too many
prisoners, and at the same time his Indian allies were letting their
savage instincts get out of hand. Bird was too humanitarian to
stand by while women and children were butchered. He turned
back to Detroit and lost Kentucky and his chance to take the
Illinois country.

It was time for Clark to give his attention to the Shawnee who
raided Kentucky from north of the Ohio River. The appeals from
Boonesborough and Bryan's Station were still fresh in his mind
when he returned from the Mississippi campaign. Furthermore,
a directive from Governor Jefferson, written as long ago as April

19, awaited him at Fort Jefferson. It dealt with the situation in Kentucky:

> Incertain whether you were near enough at Hand to afford re-
> lief, and indeed rather expecting from your last Letter received
> that you are now at the mouth of the Ohio, satisfied at the same
> time that any Plan of enterprize determined and minutely di-
> rected here would prove abortive from want of Information and
> unforeseen Difficulties and Events, I have directed the Lieu-
> tenants of the Counties of Washington, Montgomery, Botetourt,
> Rockbridge and Green-Briar to assemble and concert, and im-
> mediately with a Portion of their Militia carry an Expedition into
> the Indian Country. To communicate their determinations to the
> Lieutenants of the Counties Northward of them between the
> Blue-ridge and Allegany who are also to assemble, concert, and
> execute similar offensive Measures with their Militia either by
> concurring in the same, or undertaking a separate Expedition;
> and those again to call for aids from the Counties West of the
> Allegany. They are to give Notice of their Plans to yourself, and
> should the combination of the Enemy appear still formidable for
> their Force I have desired them to ask such Assistance as you
> can give them, and in such way as you shall Think most effectual.[9]

Clark was not sanguine about the easy recruiting of men in Kentucky. He had had experience before. But he had in Governor Jefferson's letter the authority he needed to proceed:

> Nothing is more desirable than the total suppression of Savage
> Insolence and Cruelties, and should your Affairs be in a condition
> to admit your going in Person, and taking command of the whole
> expedition—The object is of sufficient Importance to require it.
> ... I therefore leave to your Discretion and Zeal for the good of
> your Country to determine whether, and in what manner to con-
> cur in this Expedition, still considering it as so important as to
> recommend it to you, if very great Injury to the public may not
> attend the cutting you off on that Business.[10]

Clark did not wait to be asked by the lieutenants of the Kentucky counties to assist in the enterprise. He made his way to Harrodsburg and there literally impressed two hundred men into service by the simple devices of closing the land office and blocking the roads leading east—with some assistance from Colonel

Thomas Slaughter's troops. Men from the Illinois country—the Falls, Vincennes, Kaskaskia and Cahokia—came up the Ohio to rendezvous at the mouth of Licking River. They carried swivel guns and a six-pounder, with Captain Robert George as gunner. Colonel Benjamin Logan's company of skilled woodsmen joined the men from Harrodsburg. They took time to build a fort at the rendezvous, and meat for the march north was killed during the two days it took to build the fort.

On August 2, 1780, they crossed the Ohio, approximately a thousand men, most of them hardened to wilderness life and many of them with some experience in fighting the Indians. All were inflamed with hatred for the Shawnee, who had raided the Kentucky settlements almost at will and had dealt with the inhabitants, including women and children, with abominable cruelty.

Though Clark hoped to surprise the Shawnee, it was manifestly impossible to keep secret the movement of a thousand men through the wilderness. Long before they reached the first Shawnee settlement, Chillicothe, the Indians knew of their approach. But they must have underestimated the speed of Clark's advance along the Little Miami to their town, for they had to leave it hastily. Clark's spies had already brought word of the desertion of Chillicothe, and the American force was not surprised. But, though Chillicothe was devoid of Indians, it did not lack stores. There was even corn in kettles over the fires in the village. There was plenty of corn growing in the fields around Chillicothe, and there were beans. The men destroyed most of the standing corn and raided the village, looting it of everything useful to them, before setting fire to it.

Clark's spies, following the fleeing Shawnee, presently reported that the goal of the Indians was the larger village of Piqua, where they meant to make a stand. "The general conduct of the Indians ... and many other corroborating circumstances," Clark wrote late in August to Governor Jefferson, "proved their design of leading us on to their own ground and time of action." By evening of August 8, the Americans had come into sight of the town and its forts, "a plain of half a mile in width lying between us."

Indians concealed among the weeds of the prairie opened fire as soon as the Americans came within range. There was little waste of time.

> I had scarcely time to make those dispositions necessary, before the action commenced on our left wing, and in a few minutes became almost general, with a savage fierceness on both sides. The confidence the enemy had of their own strength and certain victory, or the want of generalship, occasioned several neglects, by which those advantages were taken that proved the ruin of their army, being flanked two or three different times, drove from hill to hill in a circuitous direction, for upwards of a mile and a half; at last took shelter in their strongholds and woods adjacent, when the firing ceased for about half an hour, until necessary preparations were made for dislodging them. A heavy firing again commenced, and continued severe until dark, by which time the enemy were totally routed.[11]

The Piqua battle, for all that the Indians fled and the town and corn were destroyed, was not decisive. The Indians had expected it to be, for they had been preparing to battle the Americans for some days; the Shawnee had been joined by the savage Delaware, the Wyandot, the Mingo. A French prisoner taken after the battle estimated that there were more than a thousand warriors, a figure corroborated by Henry Wilson in his later memoir of the campaign; Wilson gave the figure as 1,500. However fierce those Indians were in their raids on relatively helpless and isolated Kentucky settlements, they were no match for the woodsmen brought against them in an army.

Though the Americans took no Indian prisoners, they had a respectable number of their own wounded to care for. For some time Clark considered pursuing the Indians, but in the end he decided against it. The wounded and the diminishing of provisions militated against any further action. "I could wish to have had a small store of provisions to have enabled us to have laid waste part of the Delaware settlements, and falling in at Pittsburg, but the excessive heat, and weak diet, shew the impropriety of such a step." So he ordered a retreat, and he himself returned to Louisville, "having marched in the whole 480 miles in 31 days."

Clark was scarcely settled in once more before the old problems of payment and food rose up to plague him, as indeed, they troubled all the frontier settlements. Jefferson wrote that any campaign against Detroit, which seemed to Clark logical after the defeat of the Shawnee, would have to be abandoned for the time being; funds simply were not available. He did have ammunition to offer. "I wish it were possible to engage the Piankishaws in war against the British Indians. Should the ammunition sent and to be sent this year to the Westward be insufficient, we will send a further quantity if desired by you." [12] But provisions and money were in short supply.

The hardships of frontier life were the burden of many of the communications sent to Clark. Captain Robert George, commanding at Fort Jefferson, wrote on October 28, 1780, "We are Reduced to a Very small Number at present occasioned by Famine, Desertion and Numbers daly Dying; we have but a Very Small Quantity of provisions at present." Letters of similar nature followed Clark on a visit to Richmond, Virginia.

Vincennes suffered with the rest of the settlements. Some of the French attempted to seize a cache of goods on the Miami but failed in their purpose. J. M. P. Le Gras wrote a plaintive letter to Clark from Vincennes on December 1, reminding him again of the failure of American credit and of Clark's own:

> It is with regret I inform you of the melancholy defeat that our Frenchmen encountered at the Miami, Colonel de la Balme having started with about eighty men in order to take Baubin; and not having found this infamous scoundrel, our Frenchmen plundered the goods belonging to him. In returning they were attacked by the Miami nations who killed the bravest of them and retook the goods which belonged to the king.
>
> Colonel de la Balme was killed as well as M. Duplasy, Milliet, Cardinal, Joseph André and a number of other volunteers. Doctor Ray is a prisoner. The affair has thrown us into a good deal of consternation, for there is a great scarcity of provisions and ammunition. I pray you, if you can, to send us a barrel of powder in order to be able to sustain the honor of the state as we have done until now. I arrived from Illinois a few days since where I suffered every possible disgrace. I had accepted several notes for the provisions that you received from the inhabitants—those gentlemen took no share in the sacrifices I was making for the

United States. They fell upon me, which has taken away my last resources. I as well as Major Bosseron offered your bills of exchange which they refused. I had sent them to New Orleans as they are drawn upon Mr. Oliver Pollock. They returned unpaid. I beg you if you can to send me in place of this same bill of exchange, one of the same amount as those which are sent you from the treasury of Virginia for seventeen hundred and sixty-two dollars in order to procure me some means of ministering to my pressing wants, whilst waiting the reception of those I left at Williamsburg.

Be assured of my sincerity for the interest of the States. . . .

Major Bosseron joins me in respects to you. As he has heard that you have some bills of exchange ready made on the treasury of Virginia and as he is in want in order to pay his debts, he would beg you to send him the amount of twelve thousand *piastres* in order to fulfil the obligations he has become security for the States—and he will return to you the same quantity to make up the amount of the said bills of exchange that you may send him.[13]

But Clark was not at either the Falls or Fort Jefferson to receive Le Gras's letter but on a visit to Governor Jefferson following the reduction of Chillicothe and Piqua. At about the time Le Gras was setting forth the distress of the gentlemen loyal enough to the United States to put their own holdings up for security against the debts incurred to hold the territory for the nation, Clark reached Richmond. While letters detailing the deteriorating situation in the Illinois country were being sent to Fort Jefferson, Clark had been impressed into immediate service by Governor Jefferson; he fought under Major General Baron von Steuben as a Continental commander in Virginia, and it was past the middle of January before he was again back in Richmond, busy with his plans, which, of course, had as their goal the taking of Detroit and the ending of the Indian depredations in Kentucky.

Though the preparations being made at Fort Jefferson at Clark's order (the collecting of supplies, the making of boats) and those at Richmond (the assembling of more supplies and the allocating of funds) heartened the Illinois country, the plan offered no immediate relief for that territory. At Richmond Clark was made Brigadier General "of the forces to be embodied on an expedition westward of the Ohio," although Detroit was not mentioned.

Constant alarms came down the Wabash to Vincennes. The Shawnee and their allies, still smarting from their defeat at Piqua, were determined upon revenge and meant to level all in their path; even though Vincennes was not on their customary route into Kentucky, they intended to take and burn it. The settlers were kept in a state of alarm, the fort in readiness. At the same time, the long period of uncertainty and the lack of adequate supplies and payment combined to sow disaffection between the settlers and the soldiers, between the Indians and both. Complaints reached Clark and the government in Richmond.

Early in April 1781, Geoffrey Linctot, a major in command of the Vincennes militia, reported to Jefferson on conditions there:

> The Commission granted him on account of his sincere attachment to the cause of the United States by his Excellency, has enabled him to carry out the policy of maintaining friendly relations with the "Orebache" Indians and other tribes; but for the future maintainence of this state of things the transmission of goods, powder and other articles will be necessary. These Allies now remain true and faithful, but unless their wants are supplied, the English, who may afford them relief will succeed in engaging them on their side—The attachment of his Excellency to Virginia and her honour and interests should not permit those people to remain daily exposed to massacre on account of their fidelity to the State, for want of the necessaries of life, arms, powder &C. . . .

At the same time he wrote to Colonel George Slaughter, who was in command at Fort Jefferson, to say that he hoped he could rely upon Slaughter's "known generosity and friendship, to interest himself in behalf of a people and Country threatened with dire calamity unless promptly succoured." [14]

Matters, however, far from improving, disintegrated even further. Sometime in the course of that spring Fort Patrick Henry was without a garrison, however temporarily. On June 30, 1781, the inhabitants of Vincennes petitioned Governor Thomas Jefferson for relief, setting forth their grievances:

> . . . Since the arrival of the Virginia troops in this country; and especially since Colonel Clark left this town have we experienced

most horrible treatment from a people who professed to be friends and whom we generously received as such. But conditions have totally changed since the departure of that officer. He left in command Colonel Montgomery who, with his officers, has failed to carry out his friendly policy.

We have zealously furnished provisions and goods as far as was in our power. Colonel Clark has paid by drafts on the treasurer of Virginia which remain unpaid. The accredited officers of finance and others have assured us that continental money was of equal value with coin, and we accepted the same in good faith. When the Virginians gave us cause to be suspicious of their money, we remonstrated with Colonel Clark and the officers of the garrison, who, notwithstanding this fact, claimed for this money its value in Spanish coin. Mr. John Todd with Captain Leonard Helm, commanding the fort at this town, has caused to be published that this money be received as of equal value with specie, threatening with punishment all who refused it. As soon as we had furnished provisions and goods for this money, the Virginians appeared to think they could take by force our property, our supplies, and even the little we had reserved to keep ourselves alive. Your Excellency must also be informed, that after these first injuries, they have perpetrated others of a more serious character, by killing our cattle in the fields, and our hogs in our yards, taking our flour from the mills, and the corn in our granaries, with arms in their hands threatening all who should resist them and the destruction of the fort we built at our own expense. When they left the town they carried off the artillery, powder and balls, thereby depriving us of the only means of defending ourselves against the fury of the savages whom they have excited against us. This, then, is the manner in which the Virginians have acted in this country. This is the exact truth which your Excellency will hardly believe. This is what we charge M. Vauchères to lay before you in our behalf and to demand of your Excellency to render us the justice which is due to subjects who believed themselves citizens and friends of the States, and to make adequate return for the money we have received as of the value of specie.

We beseech your Excellency to give your command to the troops in order that they put an end to the injuries which still continue. We are unwilling longer to submit to these strange exactions incident to their lawless proceedings, and his Excellency will see that the Virginians have entirely ruined us already; and if it be thus you treat your friends, what treatment do you reserve for your enemies? [15]

The petition was signed by some of the most prominent citizens of Vincennes, among them Moses Henry, Pierre Cornoyee and three members of the militia—Major F. Bosseron, Major Geoffrey Linctot and Lieutenant Colonel J. M. P. Le Gras. Le Gras was still complaining over a month later, when he wrote from Vincennes to Clark to say that the Governor and the Council of Virginia

> have refused to pay me ... they are in doubt if your intention was to draw for hard Cash or for limber dollars. . . . I have nevertheless furnished this very day one hundred weight of flour to discharged soldiers going to the Falls of Oyo not knowing who shall pay for it; and I am every day obliged to pay Sums of Money to different people for which I was Security for the State.

He added this footnote: ". . . Having advanced all my fortune to the State I will be obliged to go again to Virginia, if not paid, or go and hide myself in Some remoted part of the world, not being able to pay my debts. . . ." [16] Clark was then at the Falls, at Louisville, and facing the possibility that the projected march upon Detroit, which had enlisted the support of both Jefferson and General George Washington, was once again not going to materialize.

Plans had been laid with great care; forces from Fort Pitt and from Virginia were to move in concert against Detroit. As early as January 18, 1781, Clark had written to Jefferson after studying his instructions,

> I dont Recollect of anything more that is Necessary Except the Mode of paying the Expences of the Garison of Dutroit, in Case of Success, as supporting our Credit among strangers may be attended with great and good Consequences and my former Experience Induce me to wish it to be the Case whare I have the Honour to Commd.

The Virginia Assembly provided money with which to pay the militia that would join Clark and indicated that more money would be provided as needed. Before January had come to an end, Clark's quartermaster had spent considerable sums on supplies, and in the meantime preparations were going forward at Fort Pitt and in Kentucky, as well as in Richmond. Food did not appear to be a problem this time; neither did boats, which were being built, and ammunition.

Indeed, everyone seemed agreed that the expedition to reduce the fort at Detroit and end the depredations of the Indians supplied from there must be made. The trouble was with the recruiting of men. With the entire Virginia and Carolina country fighting to save itself from the British moving up the coast toward Richmond, the men were not available. It was not apparent to the defenders of Virginia that Lord Cornwallis' move from Wilmington to crush Virginia was to be a rendezvous with destiny at Yorktown; men were not to be had for the campaign to take Detroit.

Besides, the Pennsylvanians and Virginians did not get along well together, basically because of rival claims to state boundaries. And Clark's anxiety about keeping the expedition as secret as possible was to no avail; the British had agents busy about Fort Pitt, who relayed to Detroit such information as they had about the preparations there and in Virginia and Kentucky as well for a major expedition, obviously one not aimed at the invading British in the Carolinas. What other goal could there be but Detroit, the source of all the frontier troubles? Finally, all attempts at secrecy were made a mockery by Patrick Henry, then a legislator, who managed to put through the Virginia Assembly that summer a resolution asking Governor Jefferson "to put a stop to the Expedition lately ordered against Detroit, and to take all necessary steps for disposing of, or applying to other uses, the stores and provisions laid in for that purpose." The legislation was not acted upon; nevertheless, Patrick Henry had foolishly announced to all that the expedition had been ordered.

The upshot of the Assembly resolution was the ruination of Clark's plans. Militiamen all too well aware of the difficulty of obtaining payment for their services saw in it a convenient loophole through which the government could escape its obligations; as a result, many of them simply went home. Nor could the damage thus done be readily repaired, for members of the Assembly were shortly in flight themselves from the invading British and had no opportunity to consider new legislation.

Nevertheless, Clark did set out. Abandoning the Virginians, he looked to Kentucky for men. He led four hundred men down the Ohio early in August—less than a third of the men he had hoped to have under his command. He expected more to join him from Kentucky. More than a hundred rangers, all Pennsylvanians, followed, but they were badly mauled by Indians under the Mohawk chief, Thayndanagea—better known as Joseph Brant—and lost to Clark. Lost, too, was his capable friend and commander of the rangers, Lieutenant Archibald Lochry, who was killed.

Even as Clark was moving down the Ohio, the effect of Patrick Henry's ill-timed resolution was dispersing the troops behind him. On August 10, John Floyd wrote from Fort Jefferson of his discouragement because "I hear the Expedition was set aside: I fear this step will be fatal to the Inhabitants here without your immediate interposition." Clark was virtually alone with his four hundred troops, abandoned behind, meeting discouragement ahead. The end of the campaign was not far in the offing.

Two weeks after reaching the Falls, Clark held a council of war with the militia colonels of the three Kentucky counties represented by the men with him. By that time, Fort Jefferson had been abandoned, and the abandonment of the fort at Vincennes loomed as a strong probability. It was obvious that the campaign against Detroit would have to be dropped; when the matter was put to a vote of the officers, the majority expressed themselves plainly against the campaign. Yet they wished, unanimously, to defend Kentucky, and they recommended that Clark maintain the post at Louisville and erect a fort at the mouth of the Kentucky River and another, if possible—and "if the same can be supported" —at the mouth of the Big Miami or Mad River. They hoped for another venture against Detroit in the spring of 1782.

The restless Clark, thwarted in his desire to take Detroit, proposed to the Kentucky county commissioners on September 5, 1781, that he undertake yet another expedition to subdue the Indians, this time heading for Sandusky.

Some strok of this sort might probably save your Country Another Season From late Occurrences I am apprehensive this will be the last piece of Service that I shall have in my power to do for you, in the Military line and Could wish it to be as Compleat as possible....[17]

The officers of the militia voted against this plan, too, promising instead to try again for Detroit in the spring. But circumstances were making that hoped-for excursion unlikely, for the events of the war in the East took a turn in favor of the Americans. Just when it seemed that the British must prevail, Lord Cornwallis was defeated and surrendered at Yorktown. The loss of his troops to the British cause, coupled with the number of attacks on Lord North's ministry in London, brought about an end to the war, and the Commander in Chief of British forces against the Americans, Sir Henry Clinton, suspended hostilities pending the signing of a peace treaty.

Lord Cornwallis surrendered on October 19, 1781. In December, the Virginia Assembly—which had formally offered Illinois County to the United States—passed a resolution forbidding the entire enterprise against Detroit and ending Clark's dream of conquest.

2

Unhappily for the Illinois country, Sir Henry Clinton's attitude and conclusions about the revolution were not shared by General Sir Frederick Haldimand, who ruled the Western Department from Quebec. From his point of view, though the original colonies might have been lost, there were still rich resources in the Mississippi Valley, and the entire area from the western boundary of the colonies to the Mississippi was still firmly in control of the British, except for the valley of the Ohio, which, from Haldimand's perspective, could be harassed and ultimately reduced by the Indians.

While the Americans gratefully accepted victory and assumed that peace had come to their young nation, Haldimand's officers, particularly Major De Peyster at Detroit, continued to urge the Indians to raid the white settlements south and west of the Ohio. Haldimand believed that concentration on and reduction of Kentucky would lay the entire western frontier of the United States open to Indian harassment. Lord Cornwallis' surrender and the ending of hostilities in the East had little effect in Kentucky or in the Illinois country; the year 1782 was no freer of Indian depredations than the previous year had been.

Indeed, General Washington trusted the British. When he complained about Indian raids, Sir Guy Carleton, who had succeeded Clinton in command, replied soothingly that reports must be exaggerated, as there was nothing left to fight about; he may have believed it himself, for Haldimand was not above duplicity. The then Governor of Virginia, Benjamin Harrison, in February 1782, declined to take part in an expedition against the Indians, for, he said, Virginia had no money for it. He added fatuously, "The Executive therefore recommend to the citizens on our frontier to use every means in their power for preserving a good understanding with the savage tribes, and to strike no blow until compelled by necessity."

The raids on Kentucky continued, and Vincennes suffered occasional deaths as a result of stealthy attacks by lone Indians or small groups venturing close enough to the fields outside the village. The American settlers suffered some disastrous raids in Kentucky, and the Indians inflicted heavy damage on the militia at Blue Licks, Kentucky; in another battle Clark's friend, Colonel William Crawford, was defeated, taken prisoner and burned to death with all the torture the Indians could devise, in reprisal for the sanguinary slaughter of Christian Delawares at Gnadenhuten.

There was nothing for it but another campaign against the Indians. Promised help from Fort Pitt—though it was later to be denied him by the Continental Secretary of War—Clark recruited men in Kentucky and late in 1782 again moved against the Shawnee at Chillicothe and Piqua. He took the Indians by surprise, but the Shawnee had little inclination to fight; they were afraid of Clark, for one thing, and they were disheartened by the uncertainties of the British, for another. The campaign resulted in no major battle and ended in a peace parley leading to an agreement that, though not signed because of the intervention of the British, was nevertheless instrumental in bringing about an end to the raids.

Early in 1783 the peace treaty between Great Britain and the United States was signed. Well before that date, Fort Patrick Henry at Vincennes had been abandoned and the defense of that settlement left to the French militia.

The Continental Congress continued efforts to secure peace, but, as most of the efforts were directed by men in the East who had little or no experience with the frontier Indians, they were often inept and bungled. George Rogers Clark was called upon to act as one of the three commissioners to seek peace with the Indians, but it was not until the commissioners met with the Indians in council at the newly built Fort Finney at the Miami in December 1785 that peace was agreed upon.

Yet a year later Indian atrocities were at a new height. Kentucky was repeatedly raided, and Vincennes was besieged, though the militia was able to hold off the Indians until two companies of infantry arrived to force the Indians to lift the siege. As Congress failed to act against the Indians, Patrick Henry, again Governor of Virginia, authorized the Kentucky militia to take action against the Indians along the Wabash. The officers of the militia promptly called upon Clark to take command of an expedition.

By September 1786, more than a thousand Kentuckians had gathered at Clarksville, the town Clark had founded across from Louisville, for a direct march into Indian country to deal drastic punishment to the Indians. The first stop along the route was Vincennes, where supplies could be delivered later.

The expedition set off under a cloud of dissension, and dissension continued at Vincennes while the men waited for supplies to follow them. By the time the supplies, delayed by low water, had reached Vincennes, some were spoiled, and rations were down to enough for three or four days. Furthermore, some of the cattle being driven to the rendezvous on hoof had gone astray and were lost. The troops were almost ten days in Vincennes, and at the end of that time some of the militia mutinied and went home. The men who were left started out from Vincennes, but their numbers were too diminished to make an effective attack on the Indian villages, and at a council of war the officers decided against the expedition and voted to return home.

Clark was mortified. Nevertheless, he thought enough of Vincennes to leave some artillery and 150 men to garrison what was left of the fort. The militia commander at Vincennes, J. M. P. Le Gras, persuaded the Indians to believe that only their French friends at Vincennes had saved them and their lands from destruction and seizure by the Big Knives, and the Indians consented to a truce.

The garrison, however illegally constituted, remained.

IV

Major Hamtramck Takes Control

After a hasty march of three days, we reached (August 2, 1796) Vincennes, on the Wabash. The eye is at first presented with an irregular savannah, eight miles in length by three in breadth, skirted by eternal forests, and sprinkled with a few trees, and abundance of umbelliferous plants, three or four feet high. Maize, tobacco, wheat, barley, squashes, and even cotton, grow in the fields around the village, which contains about fifty houses, whose cheerful white relieves the eye, after the tedious dusk and green of the woods.

These houses are placed along the left bank of the Wabash, here about two hundred feet wide, and falling, when the waters are low, twenty feet below the site of the town. The bank of the river is sloping toward the Savannah, which is a few feet lower: this slope is occasioned by the periodical floods. Each house, as is customary in Canada, stands alone, and is surrounded by a court and garden, fenced with poles. I was delighted by the sight of peach trees loaded with fruit, but was sorry to notice the thorn apple, which is found in all the cultivated places from beyond Gallipolis. Adjoining the village and river is a space, enclosed by a ditch eight feet wide, and by sharp stakes six feet high. This is called the fort, and is a sufficient safeguard against surprises from Indians.

> —*A View of the Soil and Climate of the United States of America,* by C. F. Volney, 1804, in *Early Travels in Indiana*

1

Constant disagreements and continuous quarreling within the garrison left by George Rogers Clark reached such a height that, moved by complaints from Vincennes and by reports from Secretary at War Henry Knox and Secretary of Foreign Affairs John Jay, the Continental Congress on April 24, 1787, resolved

> That the Secretary at War direct the commanding officer of the troops of the United States on the Ohio to take immediate and efficient measures for dispossessing a body of men who have in a lawless and unauthorised manner taken possession of post St. Vincents in defiance of the proclamation and authority of the United States and that he employ the whole or such of the force under his command as he shall judge necessary to effect the Object.[1]

The commander of the First Regiment of the United States Army, responsible for the protection of the frontier, was Lieutenant Colonel Josiah Harmar, who had been named to his command because his state, Pennsylvania, had furnished more men to the seven-hundred-man army called by Congress in 1784 for the purpose of manning the frontier posts and affording a measure of protection to the settlements than had any other state. Harmar had shown considerable skill in organization and in deploying his limited troops, and he had managed very well despite the carelessness with which the Congress dealt with its military commanders, particularly those at frontier outposts.

The Commonwealth of Virginia had failed to provide adequately for the protection of its western counties and in 1783 had ceded all claims to this territory to the United States. Though the Ordinance of 1787, governing the Northwest Territory and providing for a governor, a secretary and three judges appointed by Congress, was ready for passage by the Congress of the Confederation, its implementation was still in the offing, and the only government in the County of Illinois was the shadowy, unofficial one of Colonel John Todd. He had been appointed lieutenant for the County in 1778 and had established courts of criminal and civil jurisdiction for the purpose of maintaining order in the settlements. Since the cession of 1783, Todd had had no legal status.

In May 1787, Harmar, accompanied by Major John Francis Hamtramck, a short, squat man of French-Canadian origin who sat astride a horse like a frog but was a competent, well-liked officer, set out from Fort Harmar down the Ohio for the Wabash and Vincennes. From camp at the Rapids of the Ohio, Harmar wrote to Colonel Jean Marie Philippe Le Gras, whom Todd had made president of the governing body at Vincennes, and to Major François Bosseron, that he was en route to Vincennes for the purpose of protecting the inhabitants from further outrages committed by that "set of lawless banditti," which surely included some of the men Clark had left behind. He added:

> I would wish you, Gentlemen, to inform the Indians, that the United States wish to live in peace with them, and that they may not be alarmed at this movement; likewise to apprize them of troops being on their way to the Post, not a set of villains but regulars, and sent by the authority of the Grand Council of the Empire, in order to preserve good faith with them, and to protect the legal inhabitants.[2]

Le Gras replied at once, expressing his pleasure at the news and promising to meet Harmar en route.

The journey was a slow one, for it involved the movement of a considerable fleet down the Ohio, one fully supplied even with live cattle. At the end of the first week in July, the force moving west was encamped near the mouth of the Green River, which flowed into the Ohio from the south some distance above the mouth of the Wabash. There Harmar decided to march across country to Vincennes in as straight a line as possible, sending Major Hamtramck, a captain, two subalterns, a surgeon's mate, four sergeants, four corporals, ninety privates and, curiously, two musicians (who may have been buglers) around by water with the fleet.

On the morning of July 11, Harmar set out on the march with the remainder of the troops "with our cattle in the centre; in very warm weather, and the men being obliged to carry fifteen days' flour upon their backs."[3] After six days of marching in very hot,

humid weather and suffering from lack of drinking water, Harmar and his men reached Vincennes. On the night of July 17, they
encamped "near a small stockade erected by General Clarke on
the banks of the Wabash"—so much had Fort Patrick Henry
diminished since its capture at the end of that long, bitter march
from Kaskaskia—but on the following day they moved "about a
quarter of a mile higher up the Wabash" to the foot of Buntin
Street, which Harmar thought more suitable for the building of
a fort to house the garrison.

Harmar found himself in a village of four hundred houses, constructed chiefly of logs and bark, which had a population of 1,300
—900 of them French, the rest Americans. He sent his interpreter,
Barthélémi Tardiveau, to gather some information about Vincennes and its inhabitants. He reinstated the magistrates of the
settlements but made no decision about the land claims presented
by the people of the village, pending Tardiveau's report, which
was in hand before the first week in August had run its course.

Tardiveau confirmed the complaints that had been made to
Congress—"Many offences of an heinous nature"—and presented
his conclusion that most of the land claims were just, that most
of them "have obtained the sacredness of long possession and
ought . . . to be respected." He pointed out cogently that the most
difficult aspect of his task would be dealing with the Indians, and
he was moved to offer Harmar some sound advice:

> I am decidedly of opinion that no treaty of peace, likely to be
> lasting, can be made with the Indians except you are invested
> with powers energetick enough to keep the whites under sub-
> jection & call them to a severe account if, by any misconduct of
> theirs, differences shou'd arise with the savages; and I think that
> you ought to lay this matter before Congress.[4]

Though approving the reinstatement of the magistracy, Tardiveau offered some advice in that quarter as well:

> I have had many an opportunity of observing that, where a new
> settlement is made, the manners of the first inhabitants are so
> uncultivated, their principles so loose, their ideas of liberty so
> unlimited, the reins of government so slack, the voice of the laws
> so faint, that it is not till after many years that regularity, order,

peace, justice, subjection to legal authority can take place.... Above all, the French inhabitants are not ripe for a free government: their heads have been too long fashioned to despotism, to have any clear idea of civil liberty; if you restore it to them, they will find themselves in an unnatural state from which the consequent transition will be to anarchy and confusion. Cou'd the population of this country be immediately augmented by a number of respectable & well disposed men, I wou'd then be as warm an advocate for a popular government as I am now forcibly inclined to think that we want for some time a military one.

Military government seemed to him to dispose of any problem likely to arise among the inhabitants. But the Indian situation was

... very precarious.... Many numerous & warlike nations surround you: say they will come & treat of peace; but do not trust too much to their professions of friendship. The object of their visits will be to examine your strength; and, if they discover your weakness, they will harass you incessantly. If you send out detached parties, you must expect to see them cut off one after another: if you undertake a general & vigorous campaign, the enemy will either disperse & force you to retreat without performing anything; or meet you with superior advantages in numbers, in cunning, in knowledge of the country: if you remain penn'd up in a manner, in your camp, you will loose among the savage that respectability which it is essential to establish. Your poste at St. Vincennes is, undoubtedly, of great importance; but without strong garrisons at the high lands, & Wyattanons, & Miamee, it will answer nothing. Congress, I am afraid, are not well enough acquainted with this country to be sufficiently sensible of the absolute necessity of occupying those posts, without which the Indians can never be awed or gained over. Too much, or too little, has been done. You had need of at least a thousand more men, two hundred of whom cavalry.

He disparaged the militia as hardly deserving the name but suggested that it might be given military drills and its discipline improved. "You do not know, my dear sir, how soon you may have occasion for their assistance, which God forbid!" Altogether, Tardiveau's was not an encouraging report. He was, however, as sensible of the difficulty of dealing with the Indians as George

Rogers Clark had been—and as aware of the need for firmness and, above all, the threat of force.

Harmar, however, had already met with eight Piankeshaw Indians, who had come to the post as a result of the information Le Gras had sent out among the Indian tribes. Harmar had conferred with them, gifts had been exchanged and an invitation had been sent with these Indians to the chiefs of the tribes on the Wabash, inviting them to come to the post for a council. Before long, however, Harmar had a taste of Indian customs; when the last of the supplies came up the Wabash to Vincennes on August 5, having been delayed by low water, Lieutenant John Armstrong, who was in charge of the fleet, and Ensign Cornelius Ryker Sedam reported that a party of Indians had waylaid a canoe that had fallen to the rear, had killed two of the men and had taken another together with the contents of the canoe. Furthermore, when Armstrong went to bury the men, he encountered a party of Spaniards who had been harassed by Indians and saw along the shores evidence that "several large parties" of Indians were on the Wabash, very probably bent on mischief.

The Indians presently sent word that they could not come for a council for some time; it would take many days to send word to the various chiefs who should participate. Harmar took the opportunity to travel on horse to Kaskaskia in mid-August, including in his company two Indians, who supplied the party with meat. His view of the country between Vincennes and Kaskaskia differed markedly from that of Clark. He made the distance "about 160 miles" and encountered no water.

> These prairies are very extensive natural meadows, covered with long grass. One in particular which we crossed was eight leagues in breadth. They run in general North to South, and, like the ocean, as far as the eye can see, the view is terminated by the horizon. Here and there a copse of woods is interspersed. They are free from bush & underwood, and not the least vestige of their ever having been cultivated. The country is excellent for grazing, and abounds in buffalo, deer, bear, etc. It is a matter of speculation to account for the formation of the prairies. The western side of the Wabash is overflown in the spring for several miles.[5]

At Kaskaskia he talked with chieftains of the Illinois confederacy, the leaders of the Cahokia, Kaskaskia, Michigamea, Tamaroa, Peoria and Moingwena. Fewer than 200 people, old and young, lived in Kaskaskia. There were even fewer at a newer settlement, St. Philip, and nearby La Belle Fontaine—"a small stockade inhabited altogether by Americans, who have seated themselves there without authority."

Harmar went on to Cahokia, where he counted 239 people with "a decent submission & respect in their behavior." He estimated Cahokia to be "about 50 miles distant from Kaskaskia." From Cahokia he responded to an invitation from the Spanish commandant at St. Louis, Francisco Cruzat, to visit that post. He thought St. Louis [nicknamed *Pancour*] "... much the handsomest & genteelest village I have seen on the Mississippi." Then he went back the way he had come, passing the ruins of Fort Chartres, the most elaborate of the fortifications built by the French (in 1756), more than four hundred feet in length, with walls of stone and plaster. Harmar thought "it must have been a considerable formation ..., but the part next the river has been carried away by the floods & is of no consequence at present."

He remained in the area long enough to visit at Ste. Geneviève, in Spanish America, again at the invitation of the post commandant, Henri Peyroux de la Coudrienne, who was frankly interested in learning for his government about the movement of American troops in Mississippi country. On Harmar's return to Kaskaskia, the magistrates asked him to speak to the people of Kaskaskia who were assembled for that purpose. Harmar reported to Secretary Knox that he "gave them advice to regulate their militia, & obey their magistrates &c until Congress should be pleased to order a government for them." He added:

> I have to remark that all these people are entirely unacquainted with what Americans call liberty. Trial by jury, &c, they are strangers to. A commandant with a few troops to give them orders if the best form of government for them; it is what they have been accustomed to.[6]

By September 3 Harmar was back in Vincennes. When a considerable number of Piankeshaw and Wea (Ouiatenon) Indians

came in to council two days later, the soldiers already had a
fortified camp with formidable redoubts on right and left and
with a guard entrenched in the front of the camp. "The troops
wore all new clothes, and made a truly military appearance," recorded Harmar. "The Indians saluted us by firing several vollies
on the Wabash, opposite our camp. Their salute was returned by
a party of ours firing several platoons."

Harmar delivered a strong speech to the Indians. He made it
clear that the United States wished to live in peace and friendship
with them but that, if they were hostile, many men would "march
to their towns and sweep them off the face of the earth." The Indians were probably no more impressed than their predecessors
had been. They replied next day in a volley of speeches by various
chiefs, pledging undying peace and friendship with the United
States and assuring Harmar in the usual flowery language of the
Indians that their friendship would last as long as trees grew and
the waters flowed and so on. They also took the occasion to cele-
brate noisily, "drinking whiskey," as Harmar put it to Secretary
Knox in retrospect, "and dancing before our tents all the morning, to demonstrate their joy." Harmar made them the customary
presents, "to no great amount," but he was undoubtedly relieved
to see them depart for their villages on September 12.

> It was a proper tour of fatigue for me.... They are amazing
> fond of whiskey, and destroyed a considerable quantity of it. I
> trust that you may find this conference with the Indians attended
> with very little expence. I question whether the whole ... will
> cost the public more than 150 dollars.[7]

On October 1, Harmar—who had been appointed brigadier
general in August—left Vincennes. His original instructions of
May 7 left it to his judgment whether or not Vincennes was to be
maintained as a military post. Secretary at War Knox had put it:

> The leading motive to the determination will be, the considera-
> tion whether such a measure would be satisfactory to the Indians
> —and the former inhabitants; the security in case of hostility—
> how circumstanced to restrain the intrusion of lawless people—
> the facility and certainty with which the garrison could be sup-
> plied with provisions, and the price of a ration. If on enquiry into

these subjects the result should be highly favorable to the establishment of a company there, you are hereby authorized to establish a post and garrison accordingly.[8]

Harmar concluded that a military post at Vincennes was a necessity, just as the French and the British had decided before him. He had familiarized himself with the Illinois country west of Vincennes, and Vincennes was the largest settlement in it. The Indians were certainly not at the moment threatening, but the British in his view were still not to be trusted and were quite capable of continuing to spur the Indians to further trouble. The "banditti" Harmar had been sent to dislodge had learned of his coming in ample time to leave Vincennes. "I judged it expedient to leave a garrison at the post," he explained later to Secretary Knox, "as it would have been impolitic after the parade we had made, to entirely abandon the country." [9]

Major John Francis Hamtramck was left in command at Vincennes with Captain John Smith's company, numbering 55 men, and part of Captain William Ferguson's company, numbering 40 men. Hamtramck had orders to build a fort and to "regulate" the French militia so that he might have its help should the Indians become hostile. Harmar left at Fort Steuben, which had replaced Fort Nelson at the Falls of the Ohio, some additional men under the command of Captain Walter Finney and Captain John Mercer; then he went on his way back up the Ohio.

Hamtramck set about building a fort at the site of the encampment—at the foot of Buntin Street, but construction went slowly. Timber was difficult to come by. Rumors of impending trouble from the Shawnee continued to reach Vincennes. The inhabitants, too, were displeased with the magistrates and appealed to Hamtramck over their heads. By early November Hamtramck was himself appealing to Harmar:

> Our civil administration has been and is in great confusion....
> But it is to be hoped that Congress will soon establish some mode
> of government for I never saw so injudicious administration....
> In my opinion the Minister at War should have that matter determined and sincerely beg you would push it. I confess to you
> that I have been very much at lost how to act on many occassion.

He added that he was dangerously low on supplies: "My position is a very remote one, and my dependences very uncertain. If the cattle do not arrive soon the troops will have to be without meat, for my credit will fail and the people of the town will begin to think that we are a second Wabash Regiment." [10]

Actually, a government for the Northwest Territory was being formed. Even before Hamtramck wrote his letter of complaint, the Congress had chosen General Arthur St. Clair to be governor of the territory and had named Winthrop Sargent secretary. The judges—Samuel Holden Parsons, John Armstrong, Jr., and James Mitchell Varnum—were named less than a fortnight later, although Armstrong finally declined to serve and was later replaced by John Cleves Symmes. But news traveled slowly to the western colony—for the Northwest Territory was in effect the first American colony—and the post at Vincennes was occupied with matters of greater immediacy.

Information reached Hamtramck that the British were angry at the establishment of a fort at Vincennes once more, largely because such a fortified position was an obstacle to their plan for inciting the Indians against the settlements and by such means to wrest the Northwest Territory from the United States. Hamtramck learned that the garrison at Detroit had been augmented and that the notorious Joseph Brant, the Mohawk chieftain allied to the British, had been sent to foment trouble among the Miami, whose villages stood in the area of the junction of the St. Joseph and St. Marys Rivers. The Miami settlements had been much in Secretary Knox's mind as the source of trouble in the new colony; in his correspondence with Harmar, Knox had concluded that five hundred men should be established at the Miami Village "and connected by chains of post to Lake Erie, and from thence up the Lake to Cuyahoga, and from the Miami Village down the Wabash; the Indians in the neighbourhood would soon either remove or acquiesce in the system."

Brant had even more grandiose plans than the British had for him: He was intent on forming a confederacy of all the western tribes to stand against the Americans. The British had no objection. Indeed, in keeping with their duplicity, Major Robert Matthews, the commandant at Detroit, ostentatiously drew up a treaty with the Indians in which they were charged to keep the peace but also encouraged to defend their property against encroachment—which could come only from the Americans. At the same time the British were lavish with their money and gifts for Indians, in compensation for the loss of their lands, spending between $20,000 and $30,000 for this purpose and adding gifts and supplies of equal value.

Sir Guy Carleton (Lord Dorchester), Governor of Canada, did not intend to lose the revenue of the Northwest Territory. Its furs were valuable to England. Though he could not afford to have the fur trade disrupted by war, it was to his interest to keep the Americans out of the territory, which meant that the Indians had to be kept sufficiently warlike to defend their lands against the incoming Americans without the promise of outright British aid but with only the sympathy and encouragement of their old allies.

Hamtramck had to deal not only with rumors of an Indian uprising but also with other challenges closer to the fort. In Kaskaskia a meddlesome authoritarian priest, Father Pierre Huet de la Valinière, the Vicar General of Illinois, made all kinds of trouble for the inhabitants and for the military government, sending off letters of complaint to Secretary Knox and others and showing particular vindictiveness toward Barthélémi Tardiveau. From the western side of the Mississippi the Spanish government made overtures to the French inhabitants of the Illinois country, offering them free land if they cared to cross over and settle in Spanish America. Fortunately Father Gibault was still in Vincennes to keep Hamtramck informed of Valinière's activities, and the French were little inclined to become Spanish citizens, although forty or fifty families did cross to live on the west side.

The new fort was still being built when the year turned. On New Year's Day, 1788, Hamtramck detailed his difficulties in a long letter to Harmar: the rascality of Valinière; the subversion by the Spanish; the lack of clothing for some of the men, particularly of Captain Ferguson's company; the prevailing sickness (Hamtramck himself had been down with fever for some time), and the seemingly endless difficulty about supplies. "The situation of my store is about three months of flour and ten B. of beef. But

the debts that are to be paid with flour will reduce it much."
He suggested that "a very great proportion" ought to be sent to
him, pointing out that only a relatively few ill-disposed Indians

> might at any time cut off all communication for which reason I
> propose that this garrison should have at all times three months
> provision on hand and that well salted and the common supply
> might be fresh beef from the falls of the Ohio, which at any time
> may be drove in to this country.[11]

The new fort continued to rise. It was to be almost a square,
with the elevation at the main gate seventy yards in width and
the side walls approximately three quarters as long. Two-story
blockhouses, with platforms to mount cannons in the upper sto-
ries, were to occupy all four corners. Two-story officers' barracks
were to rise on each side of the sally port, which opened toward
the Wabash. One-story soldiers' barracks were to line the left
wall and both sides of the main gate. A blacksmith shop was constructed along the right wall and the magazine sunk to the eaves
into the ground behind the blockhouse at the right front corner.
The fort was to be surrounded by a palisade fourteen feet in
height, eleven feet of it above the ground.

By April 13, 1788, Hamtramck could write to Harmar: "My
piquets are up and the block houses are to their second story.
I am now in a state of deffence. If I have but provision in time I
am in no way conserned...." He had some reason for concern,
however. In mid-February a Mohawk Indian, a courier from Joseph Brant professing friendship, had passed through Vincennes
on his way to Indians south of the Ohio to ratify the peace with
the inhabitants and to assure a good understanding with the
Americans. But a small body of Cherokee arriving at Vincennes
from the south not long after informed Hamtramck that Brant
had charged them instead to prepare to move against the American settlements in the spring. The Cherokee had refused to do so.
Yet the rumors of a war with the Indians persisted.

"I know not what to believe," wrote Hamtramck. "I hear ... so
many reports that I can not forme an idea of anything. All I am
induced to believe is that if the Indians should strike it will not
be a general affaire." He recalled that in the past winter he had

learned that a party of Kickapoo Indians had raided the Illinois country from their homes on the St. Joseph River and had "killed four and tooke prisoner 12 men," which was the sort of "war" Hamtramck foresaw. He proposed to Harmar that, whenever Indians raided and took prisoners, the military in turn take prisoners from the same nation and village as the raiders and hold them hostage for the return of the prisoners. Harmar approved retaliation, leaving it to Hamtramck what form it should take.

Hamtramck had reason to complain of the "extravagance" of living in Vincennes. Flour cost $7 a hundred pounds, corn $2 a bushel, whiskey $8 a gallon, butter $1 a pound, eggs $1 a dozen, sugar $1 a pound, coffee $1.50 a pound, and the post was constantly in need, with neither enough money nor enough provisions.

At the same time, when he ought to have been about the pacification of the Indians, Hamtramck was forced to give his attention to civil matters. He was petitioned about the injustice of the local magistrates, and he found the complaint to be justified. The cost to the plaintiff of calling the court together was 180 pelts, or the equivalent of $360, a sum far too high to permit even elementary justice for most of the inhabitants. He dissolved the court forthwith and ordered the election of new magistrates. To make certain that the charges henceforth would not be excessive, he himself set the scale, subject to Harmar's approval: "One magistrate will have power to try causes not exceding fifty livers [livres] in peltry. Two ... will determine all causes not exceding one hundred livers in peltry." An appeal might be made to the district court, consisting of three magistrates, of which the senior would preside; the appellant would pay the cost of the suit. "All causes in this court shall be determined by a jury of twelve inhabitans, any person sumonond by the sheriff as a jury man who refuses or neglects to attend shall be find the price of a days labour." Hamtramck fixed all minor fees, as well, but determined that jurors would not be paid, for the jury was "an office which will be reciprocal." [12]

Though the civil troubles subsided, the Indians did not. The spring of 1788 gave ample evidence that the Indians had no attention of subsiding. Intelligence reached the new Fort Knox—

named by Harmar after the Secretary at War—that the Indians of
the Ouiatenon villages on the Tippecanoe were taking scalps almost daily in raids in Kentucky. Hamtramck, after a number of
such reports, notified the Ouiatenon that, if they did not cease
their depredations, he would take appropriate measures, beginning by prohibiting them from Vincennes. He wrote Harmar that
in his opinion these Indians would give the inhabitants and the
military a good deal of trouble "until they are distroy'd."

The Ouiatenon were not alone. In a letter to Harmar sent May
21, 1788, Hamtramck enclosed an account of two prisoners who
had escaped the Indians.

> James Gray & William Griffin Garland relate that on the morning
> of the 21st of last month [March] coming down the Ohio river
> in a Kentucky boat in company with three other men they were
> taken between the Little and Great Miami by a party of one
> hundred Indians. Forty of them were in a flatt and the others on
> shore. They were principally Shawanees, with a few Mingos and
> Cherokees. Capt. James and Camptain Snake, two Shawanees,
> appeared to be the principal men amongst them. That in the
> afternoon of the same day they took another boat with five men
> and a very considerable quantity of merchandize. The prisoners
> were divided amoungst the Indians to be taken to the different
> towns. That they two were carried up the Great Miami within
> two or three days' march of the Shawanees Towns where they
> made their escape on the 22 of April. They also say that a few
> days before they made their escape the Indians brought in a
> large quantity of plunder which they told the prisoners they got
> out of a boat they had taken near the mouth of the Great Miami
> in which was six men, five of whom they killed, the other made
> his escape.[13]

The escaped prisoners added that their captors had boasted that
they were little interested in a peace treaty, "that they prefered
war to peace as they got much more by it."

Hamtramck took the trouble, conceiving it to be his duty, to
learn the number of fighting men in the villages on the Maumee
and Wabash Rivers and also sent this information to Harmar:
In the high lands (Terre Haute) there were only 30 but at the
Maumee, also 120 miles from Vincennes, no fewer than 350; the

Kickapoo could supply a hundred men, the Ouiatenon 300, the Vermilion Indians 200 and others lesser numbers. He estimated that there were at least 1,300 Indian warriors who could engage in battle, a far greater number than the garrison at Fort Knox could hope to cope with, particularly as a majority of the men under Hamtramck's command were reluctant to re-enlist. "Not a man has yet reinlisted and imagine very few will; the soldiers dont like the place. It is too dear for them. I shall be very week in August, the time of Smith's company expiring every day." [14]

2

General Harmar was not insensitive to the difficulty of maintaining Fort Knox. He had plenty of confirmation of Indian activities, including the report of Lieutenant Edward Spear, who had been sent with dispatches to Fort Knox in April. He and his party had been attacked by Indians on the Ohio, losing two men. Harmar, however, applied to the Secretary at War for permission for the men of Hamtramck's command to draw a ration in addition to their subsistence rations, which might in some measure alleviate their complaints about the difficulty of life at Fort Knox.

He could do little about the Indians and their depredations, for General Arthur St. Clair, the Governor of the Northwest Territory, was bent upon bringing peace and order to the border country and hoped first to try pacification, bringing the Indian chieftains in for council and the signing of articles of peace.

St. Clair had assumed office under a set of instructions drawn up for his guidance by Congress, few members of which had had any direct experience in dealing with the western Indians. St. Clair was told to ascertain the temper of the Indians, to remove causes of trouble between the Indians and the settlers, to restore peace and to defend the boundaries laid down by earlier treaties —unless, of course, he could make more advantageous treaties. He was instructed to win over the chiefs with gifts and to break up any confederations among the Indians, while at the same time acquiring as much more territory from them as possible, though St. Clair quickly learned that a cession of land had only to be mentioned in order to break up a council.

St. Clair first invited the chiefs of all the tribes to meet him near Fort Pitt, which was asking most of them to come too far. They did not come. Next he set a meeting place at the Falls of the Muskingum River but moved the site to Fort Harmar. The Indians took council with their British friends on the Maumee and again failed to show up, though some Wyandot and Iroquois came and early in 1789 signed the Treaty of Fort Harmar, re-affirming earlier treaties. Most of the warlike tribes had no representation at any of the councils St. Clair arranged.

Hamtramck's reports to Harmar, which reached both Knox and St. Clair, confirmed St. Clair's growing conviction that only military action would bring the Indians to terms. Aided by the British and little impeded by the military at the posts west of Fort Pitt, the Indians could raid the American settlements almost at will. Hamtramck continued to report Indian depredations, and Harmar reported on the measures Governor St. Clair was taking, for example, the demand levied upon the Indian nations in council at the Detroit River for satisfaction as a result of the attack on Lieutenant Spear and his party.

In July Hamtramck lost some men under Indian attack. He had sent Lieutenant William Peters with 36 men down the Wabash to escort provisions up the river to Vincennes. On July 27, as the soldiers were moving back up the Wabash two miles from the Ohio, they were attacked by fifty Indians. Ten men were lost and eight more wounded, and the largest share of the provisions fell into the hands of the Indians.

> It is what I have long expected and have repeatedly protested to Major Wyllys against the mode of supplying this place. From the moment I took the command of this place I proposed to throw in provisions but twice a year, observing at the same time to Major Wyllys and the contractors, that if I was obliged to send every month to the mouth of the Wabash some accident would inevitably happen, and I have particularly pointed out to Major Wyllys and the contractor the impropriety of getting boats and men from this place to bring up the provisions from the mouth of the Wabash, for this reason, that the express who comes with the information of the coming of the provision to me always knows the business he comes upon which he tells to the inhab-

itants and of consequence is known to the Indians, who if badly disposed could at all times cut off the boats.[15]

His ability to deal with the Indians was curtailed by the same shortages that had plagued the French, British and Virginian commanders before him.

> The frequent conferences the commanding officer has at this place with the Indians for the want of a Commissioner for Indian Affairs, also the necessity of often sending expresses to the Falls, obliges me to request such things as may be presented to Indians, for it is almost impossible to part good friends unless you make them presents. They are accustomed to it and they expect it. Also a little money would be very necessary to pay for services done or things that cannot be procured without.

He added, significantly, that Jean Baptiste Constant, the interpreter among the Wea, reported that he had been at the Miami for some time "and that every day 5 & 6 scalps were brought in by those Indians, that a number of our prisoners were burnt." Constant also reported that the British sent couriers among the Indians for various purposes, all of which added up to their continuing their alliance and remaining in a position to cause trouble for the Americans.

Though Hamtramck repeatedly warned the Indians that their continued depredations would only bring trouble to them in the end, the chiefs replied that the raids were the work of their young men and that they were powerless to prevent them. The Kentuckians themselves were not disposed to be so patient. On August 18, 1788, sixty of them, led by Patrick Brown, arrived at Fort Knox. Brown had come into Kentucky in 1782, had fought in the Battle of Blue Licks in the summer of that year and had served with George Rogers Clark in an expedition against the Miami in 1780. He was a dedicated Indian fighter. Calling upon Hamtramck, he informed him that he had already that morning killed nine Indians, all of whom, Hamtramck had reason to suspect, were friendly to the Americans.

Hamtramck asked Brown by whose authority he traveled. Brown, though claiming to be acting for the governor of Kentucky, could produce neither orders nor commission. Hamtramck pointed out that he was exceeding his authority by coming into the Territory to make war; he could understand Brown's following an Indian raiding party, but such did not appear to be the case. Brown was for passing on beyond Vincennes in his search for Indians, but Hamtramck ordered him to leave and would give him no help. He demanded but did not receive six horses the Kentuckians had taken from the Indians. He forbade Brown's crossing the Wabash near Vincennes, but Brown arrogantly broke the padlocks that fastened the canoes and crossed the river where he pleased.

"I could have prevented him with the canon of the fort," Hamtramck wrote on August 31 to Harmar, "but did not think the affair of sufficient consequence to spill blood." There was yet another reason why he had to depend on "reason," which failed him:

> I had but nine men fit for duty, the American militia would not have fought them if I had been able to have marched 50 men, what French there was in town at that time would have joined me cheerfully and would have perhaps persuaded Mr. Brown to accept of my propositions.... Our garison is very sickly and no medicine.[16]

Hamtramck was forced to hold a council with the local Indians to explain that Brown was acting without authority and that his actions did not have the approval of the garrison or the Governor. Some of the Indians agreed to remain in the village; others elected to move up to Terre Haute. It was an embarrassing experience for Hamtramck, who found himself very much in the position of the Indian chiefs who admitted that they could not restrain their young braves. "I am in hopes that I have persuaded them not to revange on us," he wrote Harmar.

Despite the patience of the military, the Indians expected war, though they made many representations of peace. Their raids, however, continued. In October the Potawatomi Indians on the St. Joseph River sent word that they would like to come under the protection of the United States and that they had two hundred warriors who wished to be employed in war against the Wabash Indians, for some of the Ouiatenon Indians had killed a

Potawatomi chief some time before and the Potawatomi wanted the opportunity to avenge his death. Hamtramck did not feel that he could make a decision, though he was tempted. "I shall ammuse them until I receive your direction," he wrote Harmar.

> If you think propre to employ them under a cloack it may be done and to great advantage, but in case it should take place, I must have it in my power to supply them with ammunition and other necessarys and they must have little presents. In any case it will be advantagious to be friends with them if we should establish a fort on St. Joseph River. . . .

Harmar presently replied: "It is the height of good policy to afford them secretly every possible encouragement," which was more or less what the British were doing to their allies among the Indians north of Vincennes.

Friendly Indians were perhaps more of an immediate problem at Fort Knox than were those disposed to raiding and pillaging. Hamtramck found himself waited upon almost daily by Indians coming on business or simply to visit, sometimes in parties of fifty or more. "You well know your self," he wrote to his superior officer, "that it is impossible when fifty or hundred Indians come to you . . . to get clear of them without giving them something. . . ." He was hard put to it to oblige, but he was conservative with gifts as he had no other course. "I am of the opinion that I have not been sufficient liberal, *but you can well judge of the reason.*"

When a party of Indians came through Vincennes with white prisoners, Hamtramck felt obliged to rescue the prisoners—not in an armed action but simply by purchasing them, which made further inroads upon his provisions. Some of the provisions stolen by the Indians who had raided Lieutenant Peters' detachment on the Wabash were, however, recovered from a group of Frenchmen, who claimed to have found them hidden away yet knew they belonged to the garrison. The Frenchmen were arrested and interrogated by Captain Ferguson and four fellow officers, and the provisions were seized.

Hamtramck also found in Francis Vigo the same friendship for the American cause that George Rogers Clark had found in him.

Vigo supplied the garrison whenever it was necessary to do so, but Hamtramck was somewhat more successful in obtaining payment for him than Clark had been.

By October 1788, every officer from Governor St. Clair down to those in the garrison at Fort Knox had concluded that military action would be necessary to settle the Indians. The Governor wrote to Secretary at War Knox as early as September 14 that war with the tribes along the Wabash and west of that river could not be avoided. On October 13, Harmar wrote to Hamtramck that " a proper force must certainly be raised to chastize . . . these perfidious savages." St. Clair was all for sending out simultaneous expeditions to reduce the principal Indian towns at one time— those of the Ouiatenon, the Miami, the Cuyahoga. A thousand men would move up from Vincennes over the ninety miles to destroy the Vermilion villages.

Nevertheless, St. Clair continued to negotiate, the while preparing for some kind of military action against the Indians, whose border raids were becoming daily more intolerable. The reports from Hamtramck to Harmar and from other sources gave plenty of evidence of the burning of isolated homes; the slaughter of men, women and children; the taking of prisoners. The burden of all the reports was that the Indians could not be trusted, that, though occasionally hostilities seemed to abate for a while, the cessation could not last.

Hamtramck wrote to Harmar late in November 1788:

> I do not flater myself that they will be at perfect peace with us, for vengeance is their darling passion, and they for ever will have some old or new grudge to satisfy. . . . No length of time ever closes their wounds, let them be ever so slight, and altho' the nations should determine to be at perfect peace with us, their yong warriors in my opinion will alwais in a secret maner commit depredation unless prevented by a good chastisement.

Brown's ill-timed raid from Kentucky had cost the lives of settlers in the area defended by Fort Knox; two women and a child were slain by Indians who had lost relatives to Brown. Bands of young braves continued to raid settlements from Pittsburgh to Kaskaskia, and the Kentucky border was never at peace, though with more and more settlements rising in Kentucky Indian raids were met with increasing resistance.

The proposed council at Fort Harmar in January 1789 was a failure. None of the Wabash Indians attended, though some Wyandot and Iroquois signed the Treaty of Fort Harmar on January 9. Some six hundred Indians attended, including representatives of the Delaware, Chippewa, Ottawa, Potawatomi and Sac (or Sauk), and 27 chiefs signed the articles of the treaty, which confirmed the boundary lines between the Indian lands and those of the United States previously set down in the Treaties of Fort Stanwix in 1784 and Fort McIntosh in 1785. They left hostages against the return of prisoners they were holding. Although Governor St. Clair and Harmar believed that the treaty might divide the Indians and keep them from forming a confederacy, neither was particularly optimistic, especially as the absence of the Wabash and other neighboring Indians indicated that British propaganda had done its work against the Americans.

The Governor and several of the commanding officers were ready to carry war into Indian country, but President George Washington and his government were reluctant to initiate hostilities. The President was repeatedly impressed by the duplicity of the Indians without at first recognizing it for what it was. He was slow to recognize the part the British were playing among the Indians, for the Indian chiefs continued to send word that they had buried the hatchet, and their councils, guided by the British and American renegades, invariably resolved on peace and always deplored the actions of the young braves. But all the time bands of warriors continued to range among the settlements, killing and burning and, worse, subjecting their prisoners to unspeakable cruelty. They stole horses and sold prisoners into slavery, while the British did their best to subvert the Kentuckians, offering them freedom from raids and rich rewards if they would separate from the United States. At the same time, some disenchanted Americans in the country west of the Alleghenies were exploring the possibility of rapprochement with Britain and France, impatient with their own government's laggardliness in protecting their interests.

The year 1789 was little better for the frontier than 1788 had been; it began with bloody raids, and there was no end to them. In March Captain James Bradford and his company, 66 men in all, arrived at Fort Knox to relieve Captain Ferguson's men who did not wish to re-enlist, but the garrison's strength was not augmented. In acknowledging their arrival, Hamtramck wrote Harmar that nothing of consequence had taken place at or near the fort for some time. In the course of his letter of March 28, 1789, however, he recounted more killings by the Indians; further rumors of imminent Indian uprisings aimed again at Kentucky, and the open solicitation by Colonel George Morgan, who was busy founding New Madrid on the Spanish side of the Mississippi opposite the mouth of the Ohio, to Americans of whatever descent to come and settle in Spanish America. Morgan offered land at very low prices and appealed to settlers' prejudices, particularly their anger at Congress' having closed the Mississippi to American commerce as a concession to Spain after the Revolutionary War.

The bad disposition of the Indians was, however, increasingly evident, for all that little of what Hamtramck judged to be of consequence had taken place in the immediate vicinity of Fort Knox. Scarcely two months later, he had evidence of the temper of the savages, and that time it was plain, too, that the Indians no longer made any discrimination between the French and the Americans, as they had occasionally done in the past; only the Negroes taken by the Indians could count on their lives' being spared—"I suppose because they sell well."

He wrote urgently to Major John P. Wyllys at Fort Steuben:

> On the 16th instant, a French man who leaved on the other side of the river was killed in the night, his wife and one children were scalped and wonded. They are still a life. On the 24 four French pirogues were defeated 7 leages from here, 4 men were killed, 3 mortally wounded, one is prisoner, and the remaining made their escape to the village. The first was done by the Indians of the Rivière à l'Anguille, and the other by the Weeya [Ouiatenon].[17]

Of much more urgency, however, was Hamtramck's report that a French inhabitant in whom he had every confidence claimed that Indians had told him they meant to strike at Vincennes "at the latter end of this moon," "this moon" being in its new stage at the time of Hamtramck's writing. Although Hamtramck had found by experience that many reports of Indian activity or plans were false—sometimes deliberately, sometimes because of inflated rumors—"I think however that an officer should always prepare for the worst." The point of his appeal was, in short, the need for provisions. "I am in no ways conserned for the garrison pro- voided I have provision."

Time did not permit Hamtramck to make his appeal to Har- mar: "I never had so much business as I have had this day." It seemed to him urgently necessary that supplies be shipped at once but that every care be taken that they not fall into the hands of the Indians, who would certainly be on the watch along the Wabash between Fort Steuben and Fort Knox. "I would have the boats not over loaded to enable them to ascent the Wabash with ease." He needed the supplies in not more than twenty days, hopefully less. He hoped too, as an afterthought, that, when Gov- ernor St. Clair paid a projected visit to Vincennes later in the summer, "he will give an other face to the affairs of this country for their situation is deplorable. A chaine of three block-houses and canons might secure the village. But this cannot be done without more troops."

Wyllys, unknown to Hamtramck, had gone east, leaving Cap- tain Joseph Asheton in command. Fortunately, Asheton opened Hamtramck's letter. On May 31 he wrote to assure Hamtramck that his express of May 27 was being answered at once and that the supplies Hamtramck needed would arrive at Fort Knox within the time specified. Indeed, they had been dispatched from Fort Steuben at the Falls the previous day with an escort headed by Lieutenant John Armstrong, who found considerable evidence of Indians and was fearful of ambush, which a meeting with a de- tachment from Fort Knox under Lieutenant Dirck Schuyler may have prevented. Another detachment of villagers, commanded by Hamtramck himself, met Armstrong some ten miles below Vin- cennes to prevent any last-minute attack on the provision boats. By the time the provisions reached Fort Knox the escort was indeed impressive by frontier terms: Thirty men under Schuyler

had increased it to 73, and the militia under Hamtramck himself
had brought it to 174. "I can not close this letter," Hamtramck
wrote Harmar in mid-June, "without informing you of the cherful
disposition of the French and the few Americans I had with me.
They have in number of instances given me convincing proofs of
their attachment to the United States." [18]

The attack on Vincennes and Fort Knox failed to materialize.
Perhaps the Indians had been put off by reports from their own
scouts of the movement of provisions and the appearance of so
considerable a body of armed men. They could not have known
that there were comparatively few men at the fort at that time
but must have assumed that the garrison was very probably being
strengthened for an attack. Hamtramck had sent stiff warnings to
the Indians after learning of the impending attack on Vincennes;
now the chiefs came down to Fort Knox in person and assured
Hamtramck that they had no warlike intentions.

> They spoke to me with a submition rare to be seen with Indians,
> they gived me thousans protestations of their repentance and
> they went back assuring me that all their parties at war would
> be called in. They told me that if their yong men refused to live
> amicably with us that they would leave them and come under
> the protection of the United States, in fact the French tells me
> that they never had heard the Indians speak in so humiliating
> manner.

Hamtramck, however, was properly skeptical: "I suppose that
their povrety obliges them to make friends with us." [19]

Mindful of the fact that commanders who left their garrisons
had been broken in rank, Hamtramck went to some pains to
explain:

> ...It may not be impropre for me to give my reasons. In the
> first place I had not an ounce of provision in store, second I had
> received information that an attack was premeditated on the
> village in a few days, which if it had taken place would have cut
> off any supplys I might have expected, thirdly I knew that the
> Indians were sufficiently in force to prevent Lieut. Armstrong
> from ascending and finding, that the post I occupied was not the
> key of a Medeteranian, I concluded that it was not 70 yards of

grond which was in question but that it was my duty to be where ever the greatest interest of the United States happened to be.

By that summer, intelligence reached Vincennes from the west that the Spanish Council of Ministers had agreed to permit the Americans to use the Mississippi to New Orleans for commercial purposes, subject to a duty of 15 percent, which could be reduced to only 6 percent should the Governor of Louisiana so decide in individual cases. This relaxation of the agreement between the United States and Spain brought some relief to the inhabitants of the country of the lower Ohio and the upper Mississippi; for want of markets, they had been constantly apprehensive that their produce would be lost. This act also had one other, perhaps unforeseen, effect: It considerably diminished the movement of Americans to the Spanish bank of the Mississippi, though there existed two schools of thought about this emigration. The more astute and farseeing men in the government were inclined to believe that, no matter where the Americans went, they would not cease to be Americans, which might serve the United States well when the time came to deal with Spain about the land west of the Mississippi.

Despite the protestations of the Indians, there were those frontiersmen who could no more be relied upon to keep the peace than the young bucks. Early in August Major John Hardin led a company of Kentuckians from Clarksville toward the Ouiatenon towns. Only an unforeseen engagement with a band of Shawnee and the loss of some of his horses, together with the wounding of two men, prevented Hardin from achieving his goal and perhaps setting in motion yet another round of Indian retaliatory raids.

Other Kentuckians, however, got through to the Indians. Hamtramck complained in August about the presence in Vincennes of Kentuckians returning from an expedition against the Ouiatenon Indians—more than two hundred men, who in sixteen days had managed to kill a dozen Indians. One of the Kentuckians paraded the streets with two scalps fastened to a stick. There was little Hamtramck could do but talk, because the entire chain of command from Major Hamtramck all the way to President Washington recognized that the Kentuckians acted under severe provocation. The potential trouble for the United States lay in the fact that to most Kentuckians an Indian was an Indian; few made any distinction between the friendly Piankeshaw and the death-dealing Shawnee. Hamtramck might be mortified at having to stand by and "see the authority of the United States so much sneered at and not having sufficient power to chastise the aggressors," but he knew very well that inadequate moves on the part of the government supplied the irritant that persuaded the Kentuckians to action.

General Harmar increased the garrison in September 1789 by sending Captain William McCurdy and his company with a keel-boat filled with provisions. They reached Fort Knox on September 19. Even so, Hamtramck did not feel it possible to send a small garrison to Kaskaskia, as he was petitioned to do by Father Jacobin Le Dru and John Edgar on September 14:

> The Indians are greatly more numerous than the white people, and are rather hostilely inclined ... our horses, horned cattle and corn are stole and destroyed without the power of making any effectual resistance; our houses are in ruin & decay; our lands are uncultivated; debtors absconded and absconding, our little commerce destroyed. We are apprehensive of a dearth of corn ... or what is more probable, an untimely death by the hands of savages.

They begged for "the small number of twenty men with an officer" to be stationed at Kaskaskia and to act as that settlement's defense and for the establishment of a civil court.

Failing an immediate reply, John Edgar supplemented the petition with the assurance that he would promise

> to furnish barracks and provisions for the said number of troops, that is, flour, beef, pork, salt & rum, and the very lowest prices that each of the above articles sell for in the country, untill the arrival of the governor, or untill such time as provisions may be sent them by gouvernment....[20]

Hamtramck took a month to reply. He could not promise troops, regrettably. If he were to send them he would not have enough men left to man the garrison properly. He gave his permission to elect two or three magistrates in the village "to serve until the governor arrives." In the meantime, he would pass on the petition received from the residents of Kaskaskia to General Harmar.

In a fortnight Edgar wrote again to deplore the impossibility of setting up a civil government such as Hamtramck had suggested. The people of Kaskaskia, he insisted, would simply never obey such a government without a force to assure it.

> You know better than me the dispositions of a people who have ever been subject to a military power are unacquainted with the blessings of a free government by the voice of their equals. To the commands of a superior there are no people readier to obey, but without a superior there are none more difficult to be governed.

Furthermore, Edgar reported that some dissident citizens formerly of Kaskaskia were determined to destroy his property and him personally and that unless some sort of protection were afforded him and other Kaskaskians by the government of the Northwest Territory he and other citizens had nothing to look forward to but ultimate destruction. To this plea John Rice Jones, also of Kaskaskia, added his own testimony; he said also that Father Le Dru had left Kaskaskia for St. Louis, unable to live longer in so miserable a place.

Nor were the citizens of Kaskaskia exaggerating, for the fortunes of that settlement had declined to such a degree that, although it had once been the most important settlement in the Illinois country, it was now the last. But none of the surrounding settlements was in a position to aid Kaskaskia materially. The petition to Hamtramck went on to Harmar and from Harmar to Governor St. Clair. Meanwhile, other petitions, particularly from Kentucky, were finding their way to the President.

On December 19 Secretary at War Knox wrote to Harmar, setting forth at last a firm policy:

> The President...has desired that it may be clearly understood to be his opinion that the best foundation for peace with the Indians is by establishing just and liberal treaties with them, which shall be rigidly observed on our parts, and if broken on theirs to be *effectually* punished by legal authority.

But irregular, and unauthorised expeditions involve the innocent and guilty in equal calamity, make enemies of those disposed
to be friends, disgrace government, and defeat its designs. And
further that in future it is his just expectation that no expedition
be undertaken against the Indians north west of the Ohio, but
with the approbation of the Governor of the said Territory, and
the commanding officer of the federal troops, who are particularly
instructed on this subject.[21]

To that end one further attempt was to be made to persuade
the Wabash Indians to sign a general treaty. It was, believed
Knox, "a requisite preliminary to almost any measures of government," for "if an invitation be made for peace and they should
refuse, and still continue their depredations, the difficulties which
at present exist, will be obviated, and chastisement must follow."

President Washington also wrote to Governor St. Clair and
charged him personally with ascertaining the temper of the Wabash Indians; if possible, peace was to be established by treaty,
but if that were not possible, war was the only alternative.

The Governor, who had been delaying his visit to the Northwest Territory, could no longer do so, in view of President Washington's order. The citizens of that Territory had been waiting
upon him for a long time and were anxious to present their
grievances to him in person. On January 2, 1790, St. Clair reached
Fort Washington, where Brigadier General Harmar made his
headquarters. He spent some days in discussion and studying
maps, laying out Hamilton County and naming the settlement
clustered around Fort Washington "Cincinnati." Then, on January 5, he left with an escort of fifty men and Major John P. Wyllys.
They made good time down the Ohio and passed through the
wilderness without incident; they reached Fort Steuben at Clarksville on January 8.

There St. Clair remained for almost a month. He busied himself with a study of the Territory and draw up a speech to be
delivered to the Indians in council. This speech, with a covering
letter, he sent to Major Hamtramck on January 23, instructing
him to forward the speech to the Indians, preferably by the hand
of a French inhabitant familiar with them who could transmit
the speech to the Wabash and Miami in French, so that it could

the more readily be translated for the Indians. Though he expected the speech to be sent on its way to the Wabash and Miami without delay, he was not well enough informed about the pattern of Indian life to know that at that season the Indians were out hunting. The speech had to be made to the chiefs and warriors, all of whom were on the seasonal hunt; they also had to have time to deliberate on its propositions, which were simple enough: a demand for assurance of peace and friendship from the Indians, which, should it fail, would in turn have to be replaced with some form of chastisement to bring the Indians forcibly to peace.

Governor St. Clair was at Kaskaskia before Hamtramck's letter to Secretary Winthrop Sargent, setting forth the reason for the delay in presenting his speech to the Indians, reached him. Hamtramck did, however, send word to the Indian villages that a message from the Governor would be dispatched to them, urging that the chiefs and warriors gather to receive the Governor's messenger and to hear what he had to say to them. The Governor had no choice but to wait upon the result of his message; it was, in effect, his last attempt at peace. Should it fail, he had already decided that an expedition must move against the Indians to subdue them.

In the meantime, there was plenty for him to do at Kaskaskia. Conditions there were deplorable. Four successive crops had been destroyed—three by inundation from the Mississippi, one by frost. As the Virginians had flooded the town with money that was later disavowed by the government of that state, the citizens lacked any considerable money with which to buy food. St. Clair had sent a boatload of corn to Vincennes, the citizens of which paid for it, thus alleviating the starvation in that village. But he could do little for the Kaskaskians, except establish a civil government. He laid out St. Clair County, and Kaskaskia was made the county seat.

On March 16, Major Hamtramck deemed it timely to send the Governor's message to the Indians. He dispatched Captain Pierre Gamelin with it. Gamelin was a member of an old French family and knew the country. He did not get far, however; when he reached the Vermilion Indians who lived along the Vermilion

River, a tributary to the Wabash, his life was threatened by one of his personal enemies. He realized that, if he penetrated farther into Indian country, he would very probably be followed and slain. He therefore went back to Vincennes, reporting without delay to Hamtramck.

Hamtramck immediately sent out Antoine Gamelin, who was far more widely known among the Indians, most of whom considered him their friend. He set out on April 5, bound for the major settlements of the Miami at the place where Fort Wayne would presently rise. His first stop was at the Kickapoo village, where Chief Crooked Legs was an old friend. The tribe was detached from the main body of the Kickapoo to the north, and, being close to Fort Knox, was friendly. Its members received Gamelin with pleasure and treated him well, listening to what he had to say and promising to keep the peace.

Gamelin's reception elsewhere, however, was marked by suspicion and bad manners. He went on to the Vermilion River country, stopping first at a village of Piankeshaw, who, having learned from Hamtramck's earlier messenger that a letter from the Governor was on the way, were ready to listen to Gamelin. All their chiefs and warriors had come in from the hunt. They heard Gamelin but concluded amid many protestations of friendship that they could not give the Governor an answer until they had talked to their brothers, the Miami. The chief, however, warned Gamelin that the Lake Indians and the Shawnee were likely to give him trouble, for they were much under the influence of the redcoats. In any event, they suggested, after he had talked with the Miami, they would be pleased if he came back among them to tell them what the Miami had decided to do in response to the Governor's message.

Gamelin went on. On April 10 he met a war party of Kickapoo bound against the Chickasaw. He suggested that its members stop at Vincennes on the way and greet Major Hamtramck at Fort Knox. On April 11 he came to a large Kickapoo village, where he read the Governor's letter to a council of chiefs and warriors and presented two belts of white wampum. These Kickapoo, however, were distinctly unfriendly, if not threatening. They complained about the Governor's language, and indeed the Governor had minced no words. He told the Indians bluntly that they could accept or reject his offer of peace, with the patent implication that there would not be another offer. Gamelin softened the Governor's words. Then the Indians complained that he brought no gifts. They gave him no satisfactory answer, unless their promise that he could go on his way in safety was satisfactory. As for making any sort of decision, they could not, for such a decision was the right only of the owners of the land to make, and the Ouiatenon owned it.

Gamelin was frustrated at every turn. He was treated coldly, sometimes politely, sometimes with chilly disdain. When the Ouiatenon, or Wea, Indians had assembled with the Kickapoo on April 14, Gamelin once again read the Governor's letter. Once more he was told, ominously, that neither the Ouiatenon nor the Kickapoo could give him an answer for the Governor without knowing the decision of the Miami. Once more he was told to go on to the town of the Miami and learn from them what the decision must be; then he should come back and let the Ouiatenon and Kickapoo know, so that they could make a similar decision. The older chiefs spoke out plainly and said that the younger men were much influenced by the British at Detroit and could not be restrained. Gamelin was told too that the Indians were never given anything by the Americans, and he was asked insolently if Governor St. Clair's legs were broken that he could not visit them in person.

Four days later Gamelin was accorded a somewhat friendlier reception at the Eel River, where the warriors present expressed themselves pleased with the Governor's letter but evaded answering it. They did provide an escort to see him to the principal settlement of the Miami. He reached there on April 23.

On the following day he addressed a council of Miami, Shawnee and Delaware and again read St. Clair's letter. Such traders—English and French—as were in the village were also invited to hear what the Governor had written. Gamelin presented each nation represented with two belts of wampum and reminded them all of the treaty signed at Muskingum.

The assembled Indians were quick to deny that they had signed any treaty, claiming that any Indian who had done so had signed without the consent or even the knowledge of the tribe. Nevertheless, pressed Gamelin, the primary purpose of his visit now was to establish peace before it was too late; the Governor was intent upon it and would not answer for the consequences if the tribes were reluctant. He reminded the Indians of the many depredations they had committed in Kentucky, but he got nowhere. The principal chief of the Miami privately told Gamelin that those depredations had been conducted by the Shawnee and that the Miami had never been near the Ohio River. Blue Jacket, the Shawnee chief, on the following day virtuously insisted that the raids had been conducted by the Miami and that the Shawnee were innocent.

Blue Jacket also returned the wampum Gamelin had given his tribe. He announced to Gamelin that he had sent a messenger to Detroit to inform the British and to seek their advice. Le Gris, the principal Miami chieftain, also told Gamelin that he could not reply to the Governor's invitation until the Miami had taken council with the Lake Indians and with the British at Detroit. Blue Jacket insisted that Gamelin himself go to Detroit and talk with the commandant there, which Gamelin declined to do, saying that his orders were to go no farther than this place.

All around him Gamelin observed hostility and curiously suspicious incidents. There were Wyandot Indians at the council house carrying belts of wampum, but no hint of their mission was allowed to reach Gamelin. There were even representatives of the Five Nations present, conferring with the Miami and the Shawnee, but the subject of their conference was also kept from Gamelin, who concluded reasonably enough that the Indians were discussing matters inimical to the United States.

At a grand council of the Indians on April 29, Gamelin told the Indians that he had no more to say to them, that he had accomplished his mission and that he did not intend to travel deeper into their country. He again asked for a formal answer to the Governor's message; he was again and finally refused such an answer, though the chiefs present promised that within thirty days they would send word to Vincennes, in writing, of their decision.

On May 2 Gamelin retraced his steps, once again visiting the tribes he had visited on his journey to the Miami. He found hostility everywhere. He found evidence wherever he cared to look that the British supplied arms and ammunition and some spirits to the Indians and that the American squatters who came into the Indian lands north of the Ohio continually irritated the Indians, who looked upon their invasion as proof of the unreliability of the American government. The prospect of peace with the Indians was even more remote than before.

Even before Gamelin reached Fort Knox with his report, increasingly disquieting matters were being brought to Governor St. Clair's attention—boats captured on nearby rivers, men slain at their work, isolated travelers killed and scalped, travelers on the Ohio ambushed and murdered. At the same time Major Hamtramck was sending reports of similar outrages to Harmar and suggesting that if his commanding officer intended to continue a garrison at Fort Knox the following summer "the old troops are the best carculated [calculated], for they are in some measure use to the climate."

Gamelin returned to Vincennes on May 16, and, immediately upon hearing his report, Hamtramck wrote hastily to Harmar, for Captain John Armstrong, who had been on a mission for Secretary at War Knox, was on his way to headquarters and could take the letter with him. He summarized Gamelin's experience and added his own conclusions:

> The Indians of the Wabash would not come into any measures without first knowing what the Miami would do, and the Miami would not give any answer untill they had consulted the British at Detroit, *so the matter stands.* Those excuses are unfavorable omens, for they certainly are acquainted with each others sentiments and I think that a war seems inevitable.

As if to give point to his judgment, he also reported:

> Three days after the messenger had left the Miami, an American was burnt there, and some merchants who are lately arrived from above informs me, that as soon as the Governor's messenger had repassed, they all went to Kentucky. There is also a party of Ottawas from Michilimackinack in Kentucky and many Potawatamies. Capt. Bradford is down the Wabash with forty men,

escorting a band which is coming up, and as soon as he arrives
I am to send forty men to the Illinois to escort His Excellency
to the Post.[22]

In those circumstances, Governor St. Clair did not make it to
Vincennes. On receiving Hamtramck's message, he set out for
Clarksville and Fort Steuben; from there he detached Secretary
of the Territory Winthrop Sargent and sent him to Vincennes in
his place, with full authority to act on his behalf. Sargent set up
Knox County—bounded by the Canadian border on the north, the
Great Miami River on the east, the Ohio River to the site of Fort
Massac on the south, the eastern boundary of St. Clair County
and the Illinois River to its junction with the Chicago and Kanka-
kee Rivers and a line due north to Canada on the west. The
county took in all Indiana; large parts of Illinois, Wisconsin and
Michigan, and a smaller part of Ohio. Sargent designated Vincennes
as its capital and appointed John Small sheriff of the new county,
Francis Vigo and Henry VanderBurgh majors of the militia, five
other inhabitants captains, four lieutenants, four more ensigns
and one adjutant. He also laid down some new laws for people
entering the territory.

Meanwhile, Governor St. Clair made all speed back to Cincinnati to prepare for war against the Wabash Indians and their
allies.

3

St. Clair went into conference with General Harmar at Fort
Washington. The Governor had congressional authority to call
out the militias of Virginia and Pennsylvania, and he proceeded
to issue the call. He was determined that the Indians would be
soundly defeated and brought to their knees.

Major Hamtramck was promptly informed of the part he and
his garrison from Fort Knox were to play. On July 15, two days
after the Governor's arrival from Fort Steuben, Harmar wrote to
Hamtramck:

...We are... planning an expedition against them, to go forward from hence about the 1st October—300 Kentucky militia

will be ordered to join you at the post, which with your regular force, and the French militia, will make in the whole I suppose nearly 500 men.

The contractor assures me he will make the necessary arrangements respecting provisions, and packhorses. With this force you are to strike either at Vermillion, L'Anguille, or if you should judge it any way practicable, the Weea [Ouiatenon] Towns. At any rate, I expect you will manouvre in such a manner as to divert the attention of the Miamis to that quarter, whilst I shall use all possible means to destroy their village, as I hope to be furnished with the means to carry on a serious expedition against them. You will make every preparation to start before me; for this purpose it will be necessary that you move on the 25th September. If I should prove successful at the Miami Village, & you at the Weas, Vermillion, or L'Anguille, I would wish you to endeavor to communicate with me, not in writing, but by means of some trusty Frenchman or other, so that we may concert further operations.[23]

Hamtramck received word of the intended stroke against the Indians with pleasure. He wrote Harmar at once that it was "high time" such an expedition was made. He thought the number of men to be sent him sufficient to engage the Indians, "but if I should be obliged to keep in that part of the country until I have heard from you, I am apprehensive that I should not come off so safe." He would need more men to counter the Indians there, whose warriors, he estimated from Intelligence, numbered at least 750, a force larger than any Hamtramck could bring against them. Before setting out on the expedition, he would need cartridges, for "there is no more than 195 doz.... on hand that we want near 40,000 for I should suppose that 75 per man would not be too much."

Meanwhile, some alarm spread among the Indians and rippled up to Detroit, where the British guessed that the United States was growing short of patience. The calling up of the Virginia and Pennsylvania militia could hardly go unnoticed by those travelers to the frontier who had no qualms about passing on such information. In mid-August some alarmed Indians appeared at Fort Knox, declaring their intention to make peace. They were Potawatomi and Ouiatenon. The former lived near the Ouiatenon and could raise a hundred fighting men; they had not previously been disposed to friendliness. Nor could Hamtramck offer them very much. He pointed out that Governor St. Clair's offer of peace had been spurned and that he himself had no authority to make a treaty with them. He suggested that they might bring in such prisoners as they had, to prove their good intentions. They left, dissatisfied. In reporting the incident to Harmar, he added naïvely: "I would have deceived them by making peace with them but it could not be done without giving them goods. That I did not have."

Harmar wrote early in September to instruct Hamtramck to use his own judgment about settling on the expedition or returning to Vincennes but in any event to report to him what his decision was. He commended Hamtramck's military discipline and congratulated him on his marriage to Nicholas Perrot's widow, Marie Josephe Édeline of Vincennes, a young woman with whom Hamtramck had been keeping company for some time. He had married her that summer, nothing daunted by the approaching expedition against the Wabash Indians.

September 30, 1790, was the date set for the beginning of the march upon the Miami and their allies. Major Hamtramck's march began on that day, though the Kentucky militia had arrived at Vincennes only the day before, under the command of Major William Whitley. Hamtramck had with him perhaps 350 men, including the Vincennes militia led by Major Henry Vander-Burgh. Ninety men, including those Kentucky militiamen who could not march north because of illness, were left to man Fort Knox. Hamtramck was not without some misgivings about the Kentucky militia, and he was short some supplies, but he marched gamely toward the Vermilion River villages in what he understood was to be primarily a diversionary action designed to draw away from the forces of the Miami some of the allies who might have been thrown against Harmar's army.

Harmar, in the meantime, had far more than misgivings about the militia. As a military man, he was appalled by the Virginia and Pennsylvania militiamen. They were either undesirably old or far too young. They had no training whatever. They lacked the most elementary paraphernalia like axes and cooking utensils.

Such arms as they carried were either in need of repair or otherwise unserviceable. If they had ever had the Revolutionary spirit, they had long since lost it, and they gave themselves over at once to an orgy of bickering and jealousy over the command, for, though Colonel John Hardin was the senior commander, the men favored Colonel Trotter, who was not above encouraging the quarrel.[24] Hamar had to resolve it by giving Hardin the over-all command of the militia and naming Trotter commander of the Kentuckians. The regulars, who numbered but 320 out of 1,453 men, were under the command of Majors John Doughty and John Wyllys. There were 868 pack horses. General Harmar could hardly have started west on September 30 without appreciable apprehension, which events soon justified.

Hamtramck and his small army reached their goal before Harmar reached his. They arrived at the Vermilion River villages on October 10. They found the Indian villages empty—not very much to their surprise, for Hamtramck knew that the Indians had been fully informed of their coming; he had written Harmar on September 21 that he was reliably told that the Miami expected Harmar and his expedition and that the Indians would therefore expect some action from Vincennes. Evidence indicated that the Indians had left some days before, and not in disorderly haste, for nothing in the way of supplies could be found. Hamtramck ordered the villages destroyed.

He wished to go on to attack the Ouiatenon, but he could not do so and return to the Vermilion in less than nine days, and he would have to do it at half-rations, for provisions were short: fourteen days' flour and ten days' beef. To go on full rations would not leave provisions for the next step, even if it were only a return to Fort Knox. The temper of the Kentucky militia had been shown on the march north—desertions had been frequent; as soon as the rumor spread among the men that a further march to the Ouiatenon was under contemplation, eleven more men promptly deserted.

Nevertheless, Hamtramck believed that, with some cooperation, he could press on. He was chagrined at not yet having met the enemy and somewhat fearful that the Indians had already gone to join the Miami against Harmar, the very thing it was his obligation to prevent. He issued an order commanding the officers of the militia to use all their influence to persuade their men to accept half-rations for the remainder of the expedition. It was soon apparent and so reported to him that the men were not responding favorably to such persuasion.

Thereupon Hamtramck summoned Major Whitley and, in the presence of Major VanderBurgh and his own captains, McCurdy and Bradford, told him bluntly that he felt himself mortified—not only for himself but for the reputation of the detachment—to have to return to Fort Knox without having had so much as a glimpse of the enemy; that he hoped to be of service to General Harmar in his advance upon the Miami, but that it could not be done if they could not march upon the Ouiatenon. He now proposed that Major Whitley dispense with persuasion and order his men to accept half-rations and, if necessary, use force to compel their obedience to the order.

But Major Whitley thought it useless to try, for he knew they would not go on half-rations to the Ouiatenon. When he had attempted to persuade them, he had paraded them, spoken to them, cajoled them and at last, exasperated at their refusal to accept half-rations, berated them for cowardice. It had been all to no avail. An order would have no more effect than to cause more desertions. It could hardly be more eloquently pointed up that the militiamen were not disciplined military men. Whitley himself was ready to go, and, in his subsequent report to Harmar, Hamtramck wrote that Whitley "at all times shew'd me every disposition to go as far as I pleased to go."

There was nothing for it but to return to Vincennes, where once again Hamtramck faced familiar problems: a shortage of flour and beef at Fort Knox and, in the village itself, a shortage of corn, much of which had been destroyed by cattle in the fields. Indeed, not one family in the village had failed to suffer some loss, and the approaching winter held little promise of relief.

Completely unaware of what was happening to Harmar and his army, on November 2 Hamtramck sent his commanding officer a report of his own expedition. In his uncertainty about the course of events, he did not know what to do about matters that

ordinarily would not have given him pause. When Indians sent by
Crooked Leg came to Fort Knox with a request that the chief be
permitted to bring his tribe near the village for the winter, Hamtramck was at a loss as to

> ... how to acte respecting the Indians. I know that many of them
> will come in the village this winter to trade. Many of them will
> be hunting about the post. For me to request the French and the
> Americans to kill them when ever they see them would be the
> means of geting the inhabitans served the same way, for they
> are out every day and are not in a state of deffence against the
> Indians. I beg you will inform me how I am to govern myself.

He had learned that his fears of the Wabash Indians' going over
to the Miami had been groundless; information had come that
they had expected Hamtramck to press on to the Ouiatenon, and
they were all waiting to do battle there when Hamtramck and his
force turned back to Vincennes.

Harmar's experience had been tragic. He had reached the
Maumee Indian towns on October 15, and, like Hamtramck at the
Vermilion River, he had found them deserted. Not an Indian
was to be seen. Yet there were signs to suggest that a large band
was somewhere in the neighborhood, evidently not yet prepared
to resist. Again like Hamtramck, Harmar decided to march on
against the Ouiatenon settlement. At that point, however, the
activity of the invisible Indians was brought sharply home: They
had made off with the army's pack horses.

Colonel Trotter and three hundred men scoured the country
for the Indians and the pack horses, but the militia was so disorderly that nothing was achieved. On the following day Colonel
Hardin with the same troops went out to search anew. His considerable detachment stumbled upon a small party of Indians
near the St. Joseph River. Even before the Indians fired a shot,
the militiamen proved what cowards they were by beginning to
run off, some of them casting aside their loaded guns. Despite
outnumbering the Indians heavily, the militia took flight and left
only a small party of disciplined regulars, of whom 22 were killed
in the ensuing battle.

For General Harmar, the event bore out all his apprehensions;

the militia was unfit to fight. He ordered the destruction of the Indian buildings around the junction of the St. Marys and St. Joseph Rivers and commanded the army to begin a retreat to Cincinnati. Unfortunately, the retreat did not continue as it had begun. Colonel Hardin was embarrassed by the disgraceful actions of the militia and believed that some action ought to be initiated to make up for it. He asked General Harmar for permission to lead the militia back to the head of the Maumee River.

In view of the militia's previous performance, Harmar ought to have forbidden the venture. Perhaps he thought that an engagement with the Indians might stiffen the militia's courage. Four hundred men went back with Hardin, marching by night. At the junction of the rivers they came upon a large band of Indians in camp on the east shore of the St. Joseph River not far from its junction with the St. Marys. There at last, thought Hardin, was an opportunity to inflict serious damage on the Indians and retrieve a little reputation for the militia. He accordingly ordered a battalion to cross the St. Marys River, circle westward and cut off the retreat of the Indians.

The undisciplined militiamen, however, were completely unable to obey orders. As if unaware that the element of surprise was necessary for the success of their mission, some of the men fired at the first Indian they saw. The encamped band was instantly aroused; the Indians separated and fled in small groups in various directions. The main body of the troops—regulars and militiamen—set off in pursuit.

The principal body of the Indians, however, had not even been in sight of the encampment on the St. Joseph. It was a large band under the leadership of a resourceful chief, Little Turtle, who had taken the measure of General Harmar's undisciplined militia in the previous battle in which the militia had fled. Little Turtle had stationed his men under the high banks of the Maumee River at a ford not far below the junction. When the pursuing soldiers, including the regulars under Major John Wyllys, started to ford the river, Little Turtle's warriors raked them with fire, killing so many that the Maumee ran red with blood. Among the dead was Major Wyllys himself. The militia, save for a small squad of cavalry led by Major Fontaine, who was himself killed, took no part in the fight; though the soldiers were near the ford, they ran once more and hurried back to Harmar's camp.

Colonel Hardin now wanted the entire army to move rapidly back against Little Turtle and his band, though there was small chance that the Indians would be waiting upon that eventuality. General Harmar, however, had had enough; he had no stomach for an even greater debacle, in view of the bad feeling that existed between the militia and the regulars, who made no secret of their contempt for the cowardly militiamen. He had had proof enough that the policy of mixing militiamen with regulars was a failure, though he had good reason to doubt that the government could readily be convinced of it. He denied Colonel Hardin's request and ordered the retreat to Cincinnati to continue, considering his army too insubordinate to be dependable.

Before the end of the month Hamtramck learned of the defeat of General Harmar's army from French visitors who came from the Ouiatenon Indians. He could hardly believe it and wrote at once to learn whether or not it was true. "I hope you will be pleased to give me the account of your expedition as soon as possible which will I hope releave not only myself from very great uneasiness but every officer of the garrison." But Harmar had already written of his operation to Hamtramck before the latter's letter reached him:

> The army under my command returned to the post [Fort Washington] on the 3d inst. [of November], having completely burned and destroyed the Miami Village and all the Omee towns with about 20,000 bushels of corn & a vast abundance of vegetables & slain upwards of 100 of their prime warriors, but not without very considerable slaughter upon our side. The loss of Major Wyllys & Lieut. Frothingham is greatly to be regretted. Our total loss was 180—75 of whom were federal troops. The savages fought desperately. [25]

This communication put the best possible face on the defeat, and Major Hamtramck was not deceived, especially as further accounts continued to come from Frenchmen who moved among the Indians.

On December 2, 1790, Major Hamtramck took it upon himself

to address Governor St. Clair. He had now had several years of
Indian warfare, and so had many other Americans, he wrote, and
it ought to be plain that punitive expeditions to the Indians were
largely useless as long as the British clung to the northern posts
that were rightfully the property of the United States, for all
that the Governor of Canada refused to recognize that fact. He
suggested that, if the Indians offered to make peace in the spring,
as they well might, no treaty be signed with them, for any offer
of peace would be a ruse devised by the British, who were forever
making mischief along the frontier. Burning Indian houses and
destroying their provisions did not really stop the Indians, who
could live easily on wild game; nor could they be overcome in a
general engagement, for they would never fight such an engagement. They fought only when all the advantages were on their
side and would, under pressure, only scatter and disappear into
the forests.

Major Hamtramck understood quite clearly that there was only
one way to end the Indian wars, and that was for the government
to set up a line of forts from Vincennes to Lake Erie, all manned
by regular army men; to be firm and unmoving with the British,
who were, after all, in illegal possession of Detroit, and not to
parley with the Indians but to dictate peace terms to them. Above
all, Hamtramck concluded, it was idealistic folly to treat the
Indians as if they were the equals of white men, for they lived
by wholly different standards and codes and in large part lacked
the humanity of the whites.

Hamtramck's counsel was sound. He knew very well, as did
every settler on the border, that the disastrous adventure General Harmar had undertaken and the defeat his army had suffered would only stir the Indians to new outbursts of vengeance.
Not a man, woman or child in the border settlements was safe,
though the Indians seldom ventured into the settlements, con-
tenting themselves with cutting down solitary travelers or work-
ers in the fields bordering the villages or with attacking parties
traveling on the rivers, who were at a disadvantage in the open
against attack from among trees and undergrowth on the banks.

Nor was Hamtramck in error. The year 1791 had hardly begun
when, on the second day of January, Indians massacred settlers

at the Big Bottoms of the Muskingum. Solitary travelers were slain everywhere along the border. The Ohio River became a particularly dangerous route to follow; the number of travelers who fell victim to the Indians there soon mounted from the scores into the hundreds. Indians increased their vigilance around the settlements, striking any unwary man, woman or child who ventured away from the houses and hurrying off with scalps and, on occasion, captives. Appeals to the forts could not be satisfied, for the regulars could not set out in pursuit of either solitary raiders or little bands of Indians, who knew the country far better than the troops and who, if the soldiers could be enticed from the fort, could eventually render it helpless before attack. Only the frontier Indian hunters, particularly those from Kentucky, were successful against the raiders—and all too frequently just as savage.

Hamtramck's counsel vanished into the official papers of Governor St. Clair; there is no evidence that the Governor passed it on to any higher authority. Besides, the Kentuckians were clamoring loudly for vengeance and threatening to disrupt the entire border with raids of their own if the government did not immediately take up arms against the Indians. The government was not averse, though General Harmar was not at all anxious to risk another venture; the government was well removed from the scene of action and was not composed in any large part of Indian fighters. Thus prodded, Governor St. Clair was ordered to recruit an army of regulars for another expedition against the western Indians, and at the same time President Washington named General Charles Scott to lead the Kentucky militia in the same action.

Before the end of that January, Hamtramck complained to Harmar that rumors continued to filter into the village of Indians gathering for attacks on the settlements, including Vincennes because of its part in the recent venture against the Wabash. At the same time, his messengers were vanishing. "The 20th of December," he wrote on January 28, "I sent an express to the Falls who has not return'd. The 15 of January I dispatched a n'other to know what had become of the first and has not yet return'd. I again send to be informed what has become of them: I suspect they have been taken prisoner." In mid-February an inhabitant of Vin-

cennes was killed only four miles from Fort Knox, and some
horses were stolen, reflecting events all along the border.

General Scott's expedition, authorized to attack the Ouiatenon
towns, was to rendezvous with Governor St. Clair in mid-May,
but St. Clair and his army of regulars were late—delayed by waiting on still another mission, this time under Colonel John Proctor,
in a vain attempt to seek peace—and the army did not set out
from the Ohio, across country, until May 23, 1791.

In the meantime, Indian alarm ran high, despite the reassur-
ances of the British from Governor Simcoe of Upper Canada down
to the post commanders. Early in June an Ouiatenon chief and
twenty of his warriors reached Fort Knox on a peace mission for
their nation; they had no authority to seek peace for any other
nation. Hamtramck listened to them tell how they had been invited by the British at Detroit to come for arms and ammunition
with which to defend themselves against the Americans moving in
from the east to fight them. Hamtramck observed that they were
reasonably well informed about American expeditions. The Ouiatenon represented by Hamtrack's visitors had rejected the British
invitation and now begged Hamtramck to prevent the American
expedition from attacking them, promising to come to Fort Knox
the next autumn and formally agree to terms of peace.

Hamtramck was not impressed. He told them, as he put it in
a letter to Harmar on June 15, 1791,

> ... that since I had been at Post Vincennes I had received re-
> peatedly messages from the Indians of the Wabash by whome
> they protested an unfeigned friendship and attachments for the U.
> States when at the same time some of their warriors were killing
> our women and children, that I was tired of such conduct on
> their parts, that they had acted more like children than men who
> should have keeped their words sacred and that I was shure the
> U. States would no more be deceived by such perfidious prom-
> isses, that if any expedition was to go against them that they were
> the only one who they had to blame for it, that nevertheless I
> would inform my great chiefe of their embassy as I could do
> nothing myself. ... I also observed to them that it appeared
> difficult to me for a single villiage to be taken under the protec-
> tion of the U. States, that it ought to be a general affair with all

the Wabash Indians, as our traders and our boats would be liable
to be insulted by the other Indians who inhabit the river, to
which the chiefe made in reply that I was right and that he himself saw the difficulties attending such a partial negotiation, that
he would go to all the nations and do everything he could to
bring the Indians into his measure. . . .[26]

In reporting this incident, Hamtramck added that he had learned
that the Lake Indians were inclined to support the Miami in
their struggle against the Americans. But by the time this intelligence reached General Harmar, Scott and St. Clair were mired
deep in the country north of the Ohio, moving slowly westward
through storm and rain and flooded country not unlike that
through which Clark had made his historic march on Vincennes.
The Scott-St. Clair expedition was not intended, however, to reduce the Indians and bring them to terms after defeat in battle;
rather it was to capture Indians—preferably women and children
—as hostages to be used in dealing with the Indians, an attempt
to force them to come to terms without doing battle. Colonel
John Hardin went along with this force as a guide, but Hamtramck was not called upon to move any part of his garrison north
this time. He and his men sat tight in Fort Knox, dubious about
the expedition and its success.

Perhaps as much to St. Clair's surprise as anyone's, the expedition did meet with a measure of success. In mid-June it surprised
some Indians in their villages, and Colonel Hardin's detachment
particularly shone in action, taking 52 prisoners. The soldiers
burned some Indian villages, and in one of the Ouiatenon towns
—with seventy houses, some well-finished and substantial, for
some French families lived with them and had introduced more
advanced methods of agriculture than the Indians had known—
they came upon documents offering ample proof of the British
participation in the Indian depredations along the border and
throughout the eastern portion of the Northwest Territory.

Having accomplished its purpose, the expedition moved down
to the Falls of the Ohio. Scott had not lost a man and had brought
in 58 prisoners. As the Indians had in the main preferred flight to
battle, not many of them had been slain. The invading army had
wrought its usual destruction of crops and provender, and Gen-

eral Scott had made one humane attempt to persuade the Indians to come in peace by sending back sixteen old women and children with a letter urging them to return and surrender and so save their towns from destruction, an attempt that failed.

Pleased by the success of the expedition, Governor St. Clair chose to send out another under General James Wilkinson. This force of five hundred men left Fort Washington on the first of August, bound directly for the Miami towns. After some difficulties in inundated country, the force came upon the home village of the Miami chief, Little Turtle, who had engaged and defeated the militia and the regulars the previous year. Once again, rather than face what might have been defeat, the Indians melted away into the woods, though half a dozen lost their lives and 34 their liberty. The expedition went on toward the Kickapoo towns but stopped short of the goal because the swamps defeated the men and wore out the horses. Once more the Americans destroyed the growing corn at Ouiatenon and then turned back. They reached the Falls of the Ohio late in August, elated at their success.

The expeditions, however, had solved nothing. They had not brought peace to the Northwest Territory or even to the border; indeed, they had succeeded only in firmly convincing the Indians that, as the British had repeatedly told them, the Americans wanted only to destroy them. As a result, they began to rally and prepare for war. Accounts of the expeditions spread among the Indian tribes and brought allies from the Lake Indians, as well as from some of the tribes to the west and northwest, to whom the Wabash Indians had pointed out that, if the Wabash were cleared of Indians, they would be next to command the attention of the Americans. At the same time, those Americans who had taken part in the expeditions of spring and summer 1791 gained the totally unwarranted impression that Indian fighting was not much of a challenge.

Hamtramck was presently notified that he and the First Regiment under his command, together with another regiment of regulars, were to take part in another major expedition against the Indians, this time not a diversionary expedition like those of Scott and Wilkinson but a very large force under Governor St.

Clair designed again to crush the Wabash Indians. He left Fort Knox under the command of Lieutenant Abner Prior.

The expedition was delayed in getting started from July 10 to September 7, for General Richard Butler, second in command to St. Clair, and the quartermaster did not reach the rendezvous at Fort Washington until September. Even before the expedition was under way, it suffered a major casualty in General Josiah Harmar, who was highly doubtful about the expedition and, unable to endure strong differences of opinion with General Butler, withdrew from the army. He had attempted to warn the officers that they were virtually certain to invite calamity with only two regiments of regular troops and the undisciplined militia, which was almost completely lacking in military experience and seemingly unable to take orders; no one had listened to him.

Hamtramck—now promoted to colonel—and the First Regiment were sent ahead to build a fort on the Big Miami 23 miles northwest of Fort Washington. The expedition's main body had not yet left when the desertions of militiamen began. And once more many guns were defective, and supplies were not delivered. Governor St. Clair, observing the rowdy and undisciplined militiamen, might have taken his previous experience to heart; he evidently did not. The expedition set out in the midst of the autumn rains. All along the way groups of militiamen deserted, striking back toward Cincinnati. Other little groups of hunters, setting out from the expedition in total disregard of orders, were cut off by bands of Indians who moved parallel to the route of the expedition and were quick to draw conclusions about the potential of this army and to pass this information ahead to the Miami.

By October 20, when the last company of the Second Regiment arrived at Cincinnati, the expedition straggled along a fifty-mile distance, with the main body of men at its head and recruits and deserters coming and going from there all the way back to Cincinnati and Fort Washington. Pack horses containing the missing provisions were also on the way. On October 31, a full company of militia mutinied and went home, making no secret of its intention to raid any provision-carrying trains it might meet. Colonel Hamtramck and his First Regiment had to be sent back to Fort Jefferson to protect the provisions moving up to the front.

The force crawled through the country, sometimes covering as much as five miles a day. Rain, flooded country, swamps and harassing Indians all combined to make the march difficult and discouraging. A less optimistic and more astute leader than Governor St. Clair might have foreseen a debacle and prevented it by ordering a retreat. But St. Clair—like Secretary at War Knox and President Washington—believed that it was necessary to defeat Little Turtle and expunge his previous victory. Perhaps St. Clair was willfully blind to the omens all around him and unwilling to concede that, despite all his efforts, he did not have with him anything, apart from the two regiments of regulars, that might be honestly called an army.

On October 3, the forces under St. Clair reached the headwaters of the Wabash. Too tired to build fortifications, they went into camp, but the topography there forced them to use a long stretch of high ground too narrow for the entire army; the regulars at the rear were separated from the militia up front. The sentinels fired frequently at what they took to be Indians, and a detachment on reconnaissance reported late at night that a large Indian army was in the neighborhood. Though this fact was known to General Butler, it was not reported to St. Clair.

The Indian force was led by Little Turtle and had kept pace with the Americans for many miles, hesitating to engage them in battle because of the reputation of the First Regiment under Colonel Hamtramck. Now, however, the regulars were behind the militia, for whom Little Turtle had only scorn, and he made the decision to attack in the morning.

During the night, the Indians took up their positions. With the coming of day, they waited while the Americans were paraded. As soon as the troops were dismissed for breakfast, the Indians attacked. The sudden, unexpected assault caused the militia to stampede toward the regulars' camp, where, though the troops were under arms and lined up for battle before the Indians closed in and began to flank them, they were much hampered by the presence of the militiamen, who interfered with the regulars, as well as with the artillery. The militiamen, paralyzed with fright, failed utterly to support the regulars, so that the attacking Indians had little trouble in picking off the gunners and the officers.

The militia was ungovernable and not only totally useless in its arrant cowardice but also dangerous to the regulars.

St. Clair at last ordered a retreat, at which the militia fled with such unseemly haste that the wounded and many arms were left behind. The retreat was a rout, but hundreds of militiamen never lived to leave the battleground. Close to six hundred men were killed or missing; almost three hundred more were wounded. The totals might have been higher had not the Indians stopped their pursuit to plunder and scalp. St. Clair himself might have been slain had he not been out of uniform and on foot.

St. Clair and what remained of his army reached Fort Washington November 8. The First Regiment alone emerged from the defeat unscathed, and Colonel Hamtramck returned to Fort Knox on December 21—but not before being arrested by Colonel William Darke for "cowardice" because he had not been active in the battle but had been convoying the provision train to the rear, as he had been ordered to do. He was at once acquitted.

4

The magnitude of St. Clair's defeat made a lasting impression on the government. Before the end of December 1791, Secretary at War Knox had devised a plan for what he expected would be a final blow against the Indians of the Wabash country. He laid this plan, which called for a well-drilled army of 5,188 men, before President Washington and asked for passage of an act calling for state enrollment and training of all able-bodied men between the ages of 18 and 45.

Though approving the plan, Washington insisted that further efforts to negotiate peace be made and authorized Rufus Putnam, Superintendent of Indian Affairs for the Northwest Territory, to make them. Plans for the organization of an army against the Indians could go forward in the meantime, and General Anthony Wayne was named in April 1792 to command it.

Putnam sent three men, including Colonel John Hardin, into the hostile Indian country under flags of truce; all were slain. He asked Hamtramck to reach the Wabash tribes and to invite them to a council at Vincennes the following autumn. Hamtramck promptly did so and found the tribes amenable; the Indians, too, had been shaken by events of the past two years. Despite the defeat of the Americans, the older leaders were wise enough to know that there would be ever more frequent invasions of the Northwest Territory and that the tide was running not with the Indians but with the Americans.

Encouraged by the American overtures, the Ouiatenon Indians sent a delegation headed by their chief, Jean Krouch, to visit the prisoners held over at Cincinnati from the Scott expedition. Krouch had been delegated to make treaties at Fort Washington, if possible, but he died there, not before making a highly favorable impression on Rufus Putnam—so favorable, indeed, that Putnam, to demonstrate the good faith of the American government, presented the visiting Indians with many gifts, restored the Indian prisoners' liberty and set out with them down the Ohio for Vincennes.

The council at Vincennes took place in September 1792. There were the customary speeches, but this time it was evident that the Indians meant them; they wanted peace and an end to hostilities, whatever the Miami wanted. The Miami did not want peace. The council moved forward without incidents to mar its progress toward the treaty that was concluded on September 27, ending hostilities with the Wabash tribes and restoring to them the prisoners captured in the expeditions of Scott and Wilkinson the previous year. Putnam, whose magnanimity had played no small part in the pacification of the Ouiatenon, persuaded sixteen of the Wabash chiefs to travel with him to Philadelphia and set off from Vincennes with them.

Fort Knox returned to its routine, which now included far fewer alarms; with peace among the Wabash Indians, savage outrages were isolated incidents. The Indians were anxious to live as brothers with the white men and demonstrated that they could control and punish the young bucks when they wanted to do so.

Neither Vincennes nor any other border fort could relax, however, as long as the Miami remained unpacified. The Miami were intransigent, rebuffing every attempt to discuss the differences between themselves and the Americans. Early in May 1792, the

Fort Sackville, the present site of Vincennes, Indiana. *State Historical Society of Wisconsin*

Fort Knox on Wabash River in 1807, Vincennes, Indiana. *State Historical Society of Wisconsin*

The mound in Vincennes where George Rogers Clark made a treaty with the Indians. *State Historical Society of Wisconsin*

Kaskaskia, Illinois natural spring on the Vincennes trace. George Rogers Clark and his forces camped around the spring for two days, February 5 and 6, 1779. *State Historical Society of Wisconsin*

Pencil sketch of view of Kaskaskia. *State Historical Society of Wisconsin*

An 1853 lithographic view of Vincennes, Indiana.

Birds-eye view of Vincennes from the courthouse tower. *State Historical Society of Wisconsin*

A Vincennes view of the Wabash. *State Historical Society of Wisconsin*

Second site of Fort Knox is five miles upstream on the Wabash.

This marker designating the first site of Fort Knox is in Vincennes at First and Buntin Streets.

A typical Vincennes pioneer house of the George Rogers Clark period. The architectural details are almost identical with those of the legendary home described in *Alice of Old Vincennes*.

This frame house in Vincennes served as the home of the first Indiana legislature. *State Historical Society of Wisconsin*

Grouseland, the home of William Henry Harrison, has been restored and designated a National Historic Landmark. *State Historical Society of Wisconsin*

Father Pierre Gibault's statue stands in front of the "Old Cathedral."

The Church of St. Francis Xavier, the "Old Cathedral," is the oldest church in Vincennes, as well as in all of Indiana. *State Historical Society of Wisconsin*

Engraved portrait of William Henry Harrison. *State Historical Society of Wisconsin*

Major General Arthur St. Clair. *State Historical Society of Wisconsin*

Tecumseh. *State Historical Society of Wisconsin*

Statue of Col. Francis Vigo on banks of Wabash River near Clark memorial.

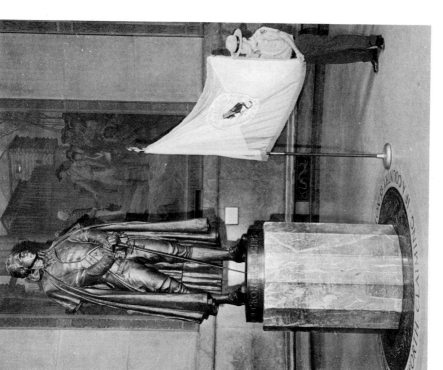

Statue of George Rogers Clark stands in front of Old Fort Sackville mural in the Clark memorial. Ranger displays U. S. Dept. of Interior's Park Service flag.

Legend on George Rogers Clark Monument.

George Rogers Clark Memorial, east exposure.

Militia Act, authorizing the conscription of the able-bodied free white citizens between 18 and 45, was passed; promptly the following month General Anthony Wayne appeared at Pittsburgh and began a rigorous program of drilling the new recruits. All that summer Wayne trained the men as they came in. He trained them in discipline, in open-order fighting, in camp making, in marksmanship, in forced marching, in maneuvering, in fortifying, in everything necessary for them to know in fighting the Indians.

All that summer too efforts to bring the Miami to council were unremitting. The Miami remained determined not to parley. They killed American messengers under the flag of truce. They scorned the advice of such Iroquois chieftains as Joseph Brant and Captain Hendrick, who had gone into the Miami country at the suggestion of President Washington to attempt to persuade them to come and talk with the Americans. In this intransigence they were supported by the British—not because the British openly or even covertly desired war, for war disturbed the fur trade, but because they still clung to the hope that support of the Miami claim to the Ohio as the eastern boundary of their lands would in time enable them to make it their own boundary, or at least establish a neutral Indian state to serve as a buffer between the Ohio and the Great Lakes.

Meanwhile, Wayne continued to train men. Late in autumn 1792, he led his army down the Ohio to a place he named "Legionville," after his forces. There was no pause in training, and Wayne acted in the conviction that the Miami would not meet in council with the Americans. So did his superiors, though President Washington still hoped for a peaceful settlement of differences. In February 1793, Lieutenant Colonel Hamtramck was ordered to join Wayne as commander of a division—the First Sub-Legion—of Wayne's army. He was relieved of the command of Fort Knox and replaced in June by Captain Thomas Pasteur.

The Miami assembled on the Maumee—two thousand warriors counseled by the British, with many British traders among them. They were not far from Detroit, and, to make British promises even more impressive to the Indians, Governor Simcoe and a company of British soldiers came down to build a fort at the rapids of the Maumee. This fort replaced Detroit as a base for supplies—ammunition as well as provisions. Information from Chief Hendrick that three American commissioners—Beverly Randolph, Benjamin Lincoln and Timothy Pickering—were prepared to meet with representative chiefs of the Miami at Sandusky at the time of the opening of buds in the spring of 1793 was coldly received. Yet the commissioners attempted repeatedly to get in touch with the Indians; they were prevented from doing so by the British, and what word came back to the commissioners in· directly was only to the effect that the Miami would not retreat from their demand for the Ohio River boundary.

That spring Wayne took his army to Cincinnati and resumed drilling there. Training continued all that summer. By the time the peace commissioners ceased their attempts to meet with the Miami, the summer had passed, and autumn had begun. On October 7, 1793, Wayne took his army from Cincinnati; in a week he reached a point six miles north of Fort Jefferson. There he was joined by a thousand Kentucky militiamen under General Scott. Wayne lost no time in putting these men through their paces, meaning to make sure that the militia would not again bring about a debacle as it had done too often before. He dismissed the men for the winter only when he had satisfied himself that they would serve under fire.

Wayne fortified his winter camp and named it "Fort Greenville." He sent an advance party ahead to the scene of the debacle St. Clair had suffered to build another fort, which he named "Fort Recovery." All this activity was observed by the Indians with mounting alarm and some frustration, for the presence of so large an army made it inadvisable for the Miami to separate and prevented the frequency of Indian raids along the border. None ventured so far to the southwest as Vincennes, and the Indians of that vicinity remained friendly, occasioning the garrison no difficulty.

Fort Knox settled back into a quiet, orderly existence. Captain Pasteur insisted upon stricter discipline than the garrison had been accustomed to under Hamtramck, but the majority of Hamtramck's men had accompanied him to fight with Wayne. Greater restrictions were placed upon the garrison; it was necessary for the soldiers to obtain formal permission to go into Vincennes, and

then they were to go only "where ... business calls them." [27] The
easy familiarity that had been maintained between the citizenry
and the garrison, largely because the French militia and the garrison were about the same business and the militiamen were in
and out of the fort, was now done with, and the garrison existed
by a far more rigid military order. Infractions were relatively
minor—drunkenness, going into the village without permission,
rowdiness and sleeping while on guard. Despite the rigidity of
the discipline, there was little insubordination, and only one desertion took place.

For a time during the winter of 1793–1794 George Rogers
Clark's younger brother William was stationed at Fort Knox as
a lieutenant in Wayne's army, but he left Vincennes as soon as
the weather permitted and went up the Ohio to join Wayne in
time for the initial engagement with the Miami and their allies.

This engagement took place at Fort Recovery. Little Turtle,
with a hard-core force of a thousand warriors, knowing that the
advance of the army into Miami country must be halted somewhere, chose to make the attempt to reduce the new fort. Unaware that the post had been reinforced, Little Turtle attacked
early in the morning of June 7, 1794. The soldiers in the fort could
see, in the attacking army, white men in red uniforms and concluded that either the British themselves or mercenaries outfitted
by them were aiding the Indians. It was a matter of little consequence, however, for Little Turtle's assault was beaten back with
heavy losses, and the Indians retreated.

Wayne continued his march by steady stages from Cincinnati
into the Miami country. On August 8 he reached the Grand
Glaize, a place of rendezvous for the Indian forces on the Maumee
River. It was obviously important to the Indians, for hundreds
of acres of land were under crude cultivation; corn and pumpkins
grew in abundance. There Wayne ordered another fort built,
naming it "Fort Defiance." The forts built at his orders were approximately what Hamtramck had urged upon the government
in his letter to Governor St. Clair some years before.

Once the fort was built and garrisoned, Wayne continued his
pursuit of the Indians, whose numbers were now greater than
those of the Americans and who fell back from the Americans

more slowly and more reluctantly once Wayne's army was in the heart of the Miami country. The Indians were ever watchful for a chance to surprise and defeat the Americans, as they had defeated the previous armies sent against them, but at the same time they were sending messengers to the British asking for military help, not only provisions and ammunition, but also men. This time, however, the British, long so voluble in promising their friendship, were strangely silent. General Wayne sent a messenger of his own to the Miami, making a last offer to treat for peace; Little Turtle, fully aware of the strength and discipline of Wayne's army, the ranks of which were not filled by untrained militiamen, was in favor of talking with Wayne and treating with him, but the British in the Miami council stood out against his doing so.

The Indians at last took a stand against the Americans at a place not far above the fort the British had built at the foot of the Maumee rapids. This site was a dense forest, where many trees had been felled by violent storms, a desirable milieu from which the Indians might fight with some advantage to themselves. On August 20, the battle of Fallen Timbers was joined. Wayne's Legion, preceded by scouts and flanked by dragoons on one side and mounted Kentucky militiamen on the other, marched directly at the Indian position, so that the battle was soon one of bayonet against tomahawk, and the Indians were in full flight. Only the forest prevented a considerable massacre. Much to the chagrin and fury of the Miami and their allies, the British at the fort remained silent; not a gun was fired at Wayne and his Legion, and not a port opened to shelter the Indians clamoring around the fort. The Americans came to within pistol shot of the fort and drove the Indians away from it.

The defeat of the Indian army was complete, and the chiefs were well aware of its magnitude and of what it foreboded. They had learned too that they could not depend upon the British for material help, no matter how many promises the British had made. The chiefs—Little Turtle, Le Gris, Blue Jacket, Captain Jonny, Buckongahelas and Tarke—turned deaf ears to the pleas of the British to continue the war with the Americans. Wayne burned and destroyed much Indian and British property and went

on back up the Maumee—pausing to build a fort Colonel Hamtramck later named "Fort Wayne"—to winter quarters at Greenville, leaving Hamtramck and his crack regiment at Fort Wayne.
Meanwhile the Indians took council among themselves, gathered
on the western shore of Lake Erie, hungry and miserable and
scantily rationed by the British.

One after another the Indian chiefs visited or sent word to the
Americans that they were willing to come for a council at Greenville in the summer of 1795. On August 3, 1795, the Treaty of
Greenville was signed. It opened much of the Miami country to
settlement, as well as a small strip of what was to become eastern
Indiana, from Fort Recovery down to the mouth of the Kentucky
River. Over a thousand Indians, representing nine nations, were
at the council, and all agreed to the terms of the treaty. Peace
seemed assured, and both the Indians and the British had failed
to achieve their goal of a boundary along the Ohio.

From Vincennes Captain Pasteur reported that hostile Indians
passed the post after Fallen Timbers, carrying their belongings
and bound for the country west of the Mississippi, foreseeing the
loss of all their land east of that river.

V

The Last Years

Vincennes stands on the east bank of the Wabash, a beautiful river, 300 yards in breadth. The site is a sandy plain, resting on gravel. No flat, subject to inundation, intervenes; and a margin of rounded stones gradually slopes to the water.... This town embraces a great extent of ground; but large gardens, near most of the houses, leave it but small claim to compactness. It is decorated with a few good buildings of frame and brick; but there are many of logs and plaster.... Every valuable or elegant improvement is recent; for although this place has been settled almost a century by the French, we have remarked that the mode of business first adopted by new settlers, long continues to operate.... Several enclosures are filled with Jimson as high as the fences; and without this notice, a view of the town would be incomplete.... At the time of determining the streets, no correct idea could have been formed, of the increase in population.... A want of sufficient room in some has accordingly been the result.... Paving has not been commenced; and though the soil is sandy, these avenues are occasionally incommoded by mud. The houses are built on different squares, but are more extended along the river. The number we should estimate between 200 and 300.... Near the town I counted seven small mounds. Adjoining these a bank and ditch remain which once belonged to a small fortress or store house, probably erected since the arrival of Europeans. All this bank of the river is beyond the reach of inundation.... Fort Knox once stood on this bank, two miles above the town; but the site is now only discoverable by excavations, remnants of old chimnies, and hewn timber scattered over the ground.

—David Thomas, *Travels Through the Western Country in the Summer of 1816*

1

Even as Wayne was reducing the Miami Confederacy, the United States government was moving on the diplomatic front to expunge the British position in the Northwest Territory. In the spring of 1794, President Washington had named Chief Justice John Jay as special envoy to Great Britain to deal with various thorny problems that had been vexing the two nations, particularly the British reluctance to honor the peace treaty of 1783 in regard to the evacuation of their forts in the Northwest.

Other British harassments had begun—British interference with neutral shipping, the impressment and imprisonment of American crews—that would inevitably lead to war if matters were not formally discussed and problems solved. Avoidance of this mounting friction was vital to American interests—not because frontier development was then a pressing issue, but rather because the American economy depended upon tariffs exacted on heavy British exports to the United States, the chief prop of Alexander Hamilton's fiscal system.

On November 19, 1794, Jay's Treaty was signed, though its terms were not published until March of the following year. Of primary interest to the frontier was the promise of British withdrawal from all forts still held in the Northwest Territory by no later than June 1, 1796. Both Jay's Treaty and the Treaty of Greenville following Wayne's defeat of the Miami were eventually to affect the fortunes of Fort Knox at Vincennes, but neither event rippled the life of the military post, which, according to Captain Thomas Pasteur's orderly book, was concerned primarily with the fulfillment of Pasteur's ideals of discipline.

In his garrison orders Pasteur had written on his arrival, June 24, 1793:

> He flatters himself that those under his Command, will readily join him with every exertion in promoting Cleanliness in & about the Garrison, one of the first objects, to presurve health, and that they will most charefully adhair strictly to the true principles of Dicipline, ... The main gate will be kept open, as Usual, from Troop, till retreat beating, the order against Soldiers going to

the Village, with the method of Gitting Water from it, will be the same as during the Command of Lt. Colo Commant Hamtramck.[1]

Nothing in the orderly book gives any evidence of the post's awareness of the world beyond Vincennes, though Wayne's campaign, of course, was of central interest. Captain Pasteur nowhere indicates it, but information must have reached the post about Wayne's success in battle. His records show a remarkable devotion to military discipline and the appropriate punishment for infractions:

> March 26th 95 On enquirey this day made into a Charge against Peter Moore, Private in the Detachment, for haveing wilfully Killed a Hog, the property of some person in or abought the Garrison, when on his post in front of the Same, It appeares that positive proofe Cannot be had to Support the Charge, but the presumption is Strong and forcable. But to lay that a side, the negligence of a Sentinell Suffering Such a peace of violence to be Commited actually on the ground of his walk, is Sufficient Cause for the Commanding to Order four dollars & a half to be Stoped out of his next three months pay the Said Peter Moore may be entitled to receive, and that the Same be paid to the right owner of the Hog, So Killed, In Conformity to the Rules & Articles of War.
>
> 12th April, 1795 Corpl Francis Lucas was this day found Guilty of gitting drunk & pirmitting the Men under his Immediate Conduck in the Village to get drunk also on the 11th Inst. It being directly in Violation of the order of the 26th day of June 93, the Commanding Officer orders Corprel Lucas Reduced to a privet Sintinel.
>
> 20th Augt. 1795. John Scamehorn Private, was this day found guilty of Mutinous conduct on the 19th Inst., being a Breach of Section the 2nd Article the 3d of the Rules and Articles of War, In consequence of which the Commanding Officer orders him 85 lashes, & directs the punishment inflicted this Evening at Roll Call, all the men off duty, will attend accordingly.
>
> 6th March, 1796. For obvious reasons, The Commanding Officer is compelled to change the limits of the Garrison towards the Village, to not more than 100 Yards to the South of West, &

South East, any Soldier found beyond those limits, without regular permission will be deemed guilty of disobediance of Orders,
& punished accordingly.

The increasing concern over boundary lines for the post's per-
sonnel reflects the growing friction between the military garrison
and the citizens of Vincennes. This friction was not without cause,
for carousing soldiers disturbed the now settled tenor of life in
the village. On one occasion a soldier broke into the local bakery,
probably in rebellion against army fare. On another a soldier un-
pleasantly accosted "a Young Lady of the Village."

Though every affront, every infraction of the rules, was punished with an almost Freudian insistence on the rules of military
life, the cleavage between the growing village and the fort inevitably increased. The soldiers were understandably restive.
Their quarters were confining. Placing Vincennes off limits only
emphasized the limitations of life in Fort Knox. There was little
room for the soldiers to grow vegetables, and there was scarcely
more for recreation within the palisade.

Captain Pasteur continued as commandant at Fort Knox until
some time in 1798, when he was directed to assume command of
the rebuilt Fort Massac. In October of that year, Governor Arthur
St. Clair published a proclamation pointing out that the Northwest Territory now held five thousand free males of voting age.
The Northwest Ordinance of 1787 declared that a territory could
elect a legislature when that number of males of voting age lived
in it. Henry VanderBurgh was one of the men elected, and, at
the first session of the territorial legislature held in Cincinnati
early in February 1799, he was chosen chairman of the Legislative
Council; William Henry Harrison, who had replaced Winthrop
Sargent as Secretary of the Territory, was elected to represent
the Territory in Congress.

The Territory, however, was not long to remain under this
government. For Ohio was admitted as a state on July 4, 1800,
which left the diminished Indiana Territory, with Vincennes as
its capital. President John Adams appointed William Henry Harrison Governor of Indiana Territory, John Gibson secretary and
Henry VanderBurgh, William Clark and John Griffin judges.

By that time there were close to 2,500 people living in and around Vincennes, including about 50 Wabash traders and 28 slaves. Close to a thousand people lived at the Falls of the Ohio, and in and around Kaskaskia and Cahokia there were over two thousand more. There were lesser settlements at Fort Massac, Prairie du Chien at the mouth of the Wisconsin, Green Bay and Peoria. Vincennes was not only the largest settlement in the new Territory but also centrally located to the majority of its population.

When Governor Harrison came to Vincennes he found the fort under the command of Captain Honest F. Johnston, with whom he was soon on amiable terms. He wrote to a friend later that year: "We have a Company of troops commanded by Honest F. Johnston of the 4th. We generally spend half the day together making war upon the partridges, grouse and fish—the latter we take in great numbers in a seine." [2] The strictures and limitations of movement imposed by Captain Pasteur evidently were not carried on by his successor.

The Governor's pleasure at hunting with so amiable a companion did not last long, however. Captain Cornelius Lyman replaced Captain Johnston in 1802. Lyman took part in the Indian council called by the Governor in August of that year. Harrison, always eager to please President Thomas Jefferson, was intent on pursuing a policy of land acquisition from the Indians and was inclined to press upon the Indians such various old claims as cessions to the Wabash and Illinois Companies, which Congress had twice declared worthless and which the Indians invariably indignantly denied.

The council at Vincennes was called as a direct result of Harrison's pressing old claims and the agitation among the Indians as this information spread among them. Secretary of War Dearborn wrote Harrison on June 17 to caution him:

> I can only say that prudence forbids our extending our claims to any such lengths as may increase any unfavorable impressions already made on the minds of the Indians. You will therefore treat the subject of the boundaries of the Treaty of Vincennes in such manner as your own judgment shall dictate under existing circumstances.[3]

Existing circumstances were not favorable. When the council opened on August 12, Harrison doggedly advanced the old claims to land ceded to the Wabash and Illinois Companies, which infuriated the Indians, who pointed out that only a decade before the United States had guaranteed them their right to refuse to sell, a guarantee reiterated in the Treaty of Greenville. It took all the persuasion of Captain William Wells, Little Turtle's son-in-law, to induce the Indians even to sign a preliminary treaty. This treaty was signed on September 17, 1802, and promised only that Little Turtle, Richardville, Topenebee and Winamac—four of the leading Wabash chiefs—would meet Harrison at Fort Wayne to conclude a final treaty in the course of the next spring. It was the best that could be done at Vincennes; the Indians, angry and suspicious at Harrison's blundering approach, would not sign a final treaty.

By early 1803, dissatisfaction with the old barracks and officers' quarters at Fort Knox had impressed the War Department—very probably through Governor Harrison, rather than Captain Lyman, for it was to Harrison that Henry Dearborn wrote on February 21 asking to know how much repairs would cost and how much new land might cost. Evidently the War Department had already decided upon removal of Fort Knox to a new location, for on April 13 Dearborn wrote directly to Captain Lyman, "When you have consulted with Govr. Harrison and decided on the most suitable Scite for a military post at Vincennes where the land can be obtained on reasonable terms, you will please to inform me accordingly, noting price pr. acre from ten to one hundred acres." [4] Subsequently the Secretary of War ordered the purchase of land, though it was manifest that the old fort must continue to be occupied for some months, as the building of the new fort could not be begun until that autumn.

Not unexpectedly, the land chosen was outside Vincennes, the citizens of which had complained increasingly about the presence of the garrison. The site for the new fort was approximately three miles up the Wabash at a rock outcropping locally known as "Petit Rocher." It sloped back from the river and was well forested. It afforded an advantageous view up and down river and commanded Vincennes, though a fort built there could hardly be looked upon as much of a defense of that village.

Negotiations moved forward without haste.

Governor Harrison's efforts to acquire the Indian lands were pressed far more impatiently. President Jefferson—to whom the Delaware chief, Buckongahelas, had written in protest against Harrison's methods—had written the Governor early in February 1803 that there seemed to him no future for the Indians in the Territory, apart from absorption into the white civilization or removal across the Mississippi. Jefferson thoroughly encouraged Harrison's goals and sent him a general commission for concluding treaties with the Indians throughout the Territory:

> The crisis is pressing. Whatever can now be obtained, must be obtained quickly. The occupation of New Orleans, hourly expected, by the French, is already felt like a light breeze by the Indians. You know the sentiments they entertain of that nation. Under the hope of their protection, they will immediately stiffen against cessions of land to us. We had better therefore do at once what can now be done.[5]

As the year advanced, it was borne in upon Harrison that many of the tribes would not honor a treaty signed only by the chiefs designated in the preliminary treaty signed at Vincennes and would not, in fact, present themselves at Fort Wayne in June. Even a majority of the Miami would not follow Little Turtle and Richardville, their own chiefs, who were ready to sign a treaty. It was not until Harrison announced that the goods and annuities to be distributed among the tribes under the Treaty of Greenville would be given only to those tribes attending the Fort Wayne council that the chiefs agreed to confer.

But the Indians were well aware of Harrison's real motive at Fort Wayne; they were not misled by his appeals for friendship and understood that what Harrison really wanted was their hunting grounds—some immediately, some later, until he had them all. The discussions at the council were bitter and protracted, and at least one major tribe, the Shawnee, stormed angrily away, refusing to sign a treaty of any kind. Eventually, however, some of the Shawnee chiefs did sign. But, like chiefs of the Miami,

Potawatomi, Delaware and Kickapoo, they signed for themselves, scorning the authority of the four chiefs who had put their names to the preliminary treaty at Vincennes.

Harrison thus achieved his first major goal. He gained for the United States over a million acres of land, all on the premise that the new treaty was only marking off the boundaries of land ceded by the Treaty of Greenville. The Indians gained nothing, except the picayune allowance of 150 bushels of salt every year. Harrison was storing up trouble for the Territory, for Indian resentment ran deep and wide.

Yet he was merely implementing Jefferson's policy without demur. Harrison was as concerned for the Indians as was Jefferson; each believed that the government should do everything possible to help the Indians to become assimilated into the white man's civilization, sending men among them to teach them what the white men knew, particularly of agriculture and establishing trading houses—but without asking whether or not the Indians were interested in adjusting to civilization. At the same time, the government was intent upon expunging the Indian land claims and pressed so incessantly that the Indians were repelled by the methods of white men and grew antipathetic to his civilization.

Having begun making treaties, Harrison continued to push his policy; he was not averse to the signing of treaties by pliable chiefs who did not represent the sentiments of the tribe or even of its important leaders. In August 1803, he wrung from the Kaskaskia Indians more than 7 million acres in lower Illinois. Late in 1804, he brought into the United States more than 50 million acres by treaty with the Sauk and Fox.[6] One after another, the Indian tribes gave up their lands, but almost every treaty that was concluded stirred up more resentment among the Indians.

Meanwhile, at Vincennes the second Fort Knox was rising on Petit Rocher. Secretary of War Dearborn wrote Captain Lyman on August 4, 1803, authorizing him to begin the building of a stockade once the land decided upon had been bought. Dearborn directed that the stockade should enclose a blockhouse, barracks for the garrison, perhaps a store and a compact powder magazine to be built of brick. The necessaries would be sent from Pittsburgh to the Falls and from there up the Wabash to Fort Knox. On the following day, J. Wingate, Jr., of the War Department, listed the articles to be forwarded: nails, broadaxes, ordinary axes, window glass, bar iron and an assortment of tools necessary to the construction of the new fort. The War Department allotted the sum of $200 to Fort Knox for fortifications, presumably the new Fort Knox—a sum as niggardly as that allowed by the French for the establishment of the first fort at Vincennes.

Construction could not begin until the supplies reached Vincennes, but on October 1, 1804, Captain Lyman was paid $25 "for drawing the deeds of a tract of land whereon the fort near Vincennes is erected." [7] The War Department instructed Captain Lyman to make as much use as possible "of any or all of the old buildings at Vincennes," that is, at the fort there, in the construction of the new fort. With a stout working force—one captain, one first lieutenant, one second lieutenant, one ensign, four sergeants, three corporals, three musicians, 39 privates and one surgeon's mate—it was far easier to cut new timber on the site of Fort Knox than to tear apart the old fort and transport the materials up the river.

Secretary of War Dearborn acknowledged receipt of the plan for the new fort on December 8, 1803. He sent back his tentative approval and set down terms of payment for the men who worked on the buildings; each was to be allowed 10 cents a day and one gill of extra spirits, and Captain Lyman was to keep a careful record of such labor and its payment.

The first requirement at the new fort was living quarters, and they were very probably the first thing built. Nor was construction very much hurried, for life in the vicinity of Vincennes was tranquil. At the same time that the second Fort Knox was rising above Vincennes, Governor Harrison was building his home, Grouseland, for which he very probably requisitioned some of the timber from the old Fort Knox. Sometime in 1805 the garrison and officers took up their new quarters on Petit Rocher, but these quarters were not stockaded.

In the following year rumors of strange activities among the Indians of the Territory began to reach Governor Harrison. He began to hear of two Shawnee brothers, twins—the Prophet Elsk-

watawa and Tecumseh—particularly of the Prophet, who had
begun to go around visiting various tribes and exhorting them to
stand up against the white men. He was not known to urge violence, but it was reported that Christian converts among the Indians and chieftains friendly to the whites (like the Delaware
Teteboxti, who had succeeded to his place at the death of Buckongahelas in 1804 and who had been among the chiefs to sign
treaties with Harrison) came to sudden ends.

This purge of Indians friendly to the Americans was ominous.
At the same time, Harrison was informed that the British were
keeping up their ties with the Northwest Indians from their fort
at Malden, across from Detroit. Indians regularly traveled to
Malden and brought back assurances of continued British friendship. The Prophet began his preaching among the Christian Delaware at Anderson, storming against the effeminacy of the Christian religion, liquor (which the Indians of the Territory found
all too easy to get, thanks to greedy and unscrupulous traders)
and the civilization of the white man. Essentially the Prophet's
teachings pointed in the direction of another confederation
against the whites, but this time its religious overtones lent it a
mystical quality lacking in all such previous confederations.

The Prophet's following grew and spread among all the tribes.
His disciples, many of them undoubtedly self-seeking and am-
bitious young braves, could be found as far west as the Missouri.
The Prophet's purge was ultimately halted by Tecumseh, who
recognized that the replacement of leading Indians friendly to
the Americans by inimical younger men was alarming the settlers
and might drive the Americans to arms against the tribes before
he had succeeded in putting together a confederation strong
enough to oppose the Americans successfully. The Prophet, however, did not diminish his efforts on behalf of the confederation,
and constant reports of his preaching and of its success based on
its mystical quality reached Harrison, who was less aware of
Tecumseh's success among the tribes. Tecumseh was less open as
he went about work for his cause.

Yet Tecumseh was more forthright and honest than either his
brother or Harrison. The Prophet preached among the Indians
but regularly sent protestations of friendship for the Americans

to Harrison, whereas the Governor, at the same time that he assured the Indians of his concern for their welfare, was bombarding the Secretary of War and the President with letters urging war against the Indians, particularly the Shawnee. Fundamentally, Harrison disliked and distrusted the Indians; his concept of them had been shaped by his contact with the Vincennes Piankeshaw, who, long since debauched by the whites, were often drunk, unclean and disorderly. Furthermore, he was motivated by the desire to extinguish all Indian claims in the Territory and hoped to see the tribes pushed west of the Mississippi. At the same time, he was obsessed with the conviction that the British were inciting the Indians, whereas the truth was that the British were doing no more than keeping up their ties with them and were actually counseling the Prophet and Tecumseh against war.

Though the Prophet was not prepossessing in appearance [8]— unlike Tecumseh, who was a stalwart Indian of striking appearance and presence—he exerted a singular influence on his followers; claiming inspiration by the Great Spirit, he played upon the Indians' natural grievances against the whites. By 1807 frontier incidents had increased, and apprehension about the Prophet's intentions had spread throughout the Territory.

Harrison made frequent representations to the Shawnee, demanding that the Prophet and his followers move, charging the Prophet with accepting the guidance of the British in his unfriendly actions against the whites. Harrison was unwilling to accept the fact that the Indians were less influenced by the British than by the depredations of the whites, which were at least as frequent as those of the Indians against the settlers. The Prophet resisted for many months, but at last early in 1808 he moved far up the Wabash into Indian country to the town of Tippecanoe.

As Tecumseh, unknown to Harrison, was frequently absent from the Territory, seeking allies as far west as the Osage on the other side of the Mississippi, Harrison naturally concluded that the Prophet, rather than Tecumseh, was the head of the confederacy. Harrison wrote him frequent letters, complaining of his friendship for the British and charging him with incitement of the young braves until, at last, the Prophet proposed to visit

Vincennes and present himself to Harrison to prove that he had an unfounded bad impression.

In August 1808 the Prophet arrived. He spent two weeks at Vincennes and saw the Governor frequently. His glibness and plausibility deceived Harrison more readily than Harrison's declarations of friendship deceived the Prophet. He earnestly asked Harrison to use all his influence to prevent liquor from reaching his people, and, on several occasions, he harangued the Indians who had accompanied him on the subject of the evils of war and liquor. Harrison was impressed enough to write to the Secretary of War in praise of the Prophet's artful handling of the Indians and of his conclusion that the Prophet's influence might be "rather advantageous than otherwise to the United States." [9]

Harrison's favorable impression of the Prophet lasted only until he received the next report from one of the spies he had constantly moving among the tribes, spies who were inclined to exaggerate every rumor and frequently to invent some of their own. The spies who reported to the Prophet and Tecumseh were more reliable than Harrison's. By early 1809 Harrison was convinced that the Prophet and his followers were contemplating an immediate attack upon the settlements. He lost no time in calling out two companies of militia, for the garrison at Fort Knox was now much reduced. Only fourteen or fifteen men under Lieutenant Ambrose Whitlock manned the fort, and the fort itself was not even surrounded by a palisade and was still without an adequate blockhouse.

The rumor, however, had come from an enemy of the Prophet's, and further reports from spies, as well as protestations from the Prophet himself, convinced Harrison that no attack was being contemplated. He dismissed the militia and sent word to the Prophet that he would like to see him. The Prophet accordingly came to Vincennes again in the summer of 1809.

This time the atmosphere was less friendly. For one thing, the administration had changed. Madison had replaced Jefferson, and Jefferson's concern with the western lands was not shared by Madison, who was considerably more taken up with foreign affairs, particularly relations with Great Britain. Secretary of War William Eustis, however, took a strictly military view of the Indian problem, for he lacked either diplomacy or humanitarianism. For another, one of Harrison's least trustworthy agents had spread the rumor that the Prophet and Tecumseh planned to wipe out Vincennes and other white settlements one after the other, a creation of his own imagination but a tale Harrison readily believed. He blamed the supposed Indian plan on the British.

The Prophet protested his innocence. He insisted that no such plan had ever crossed his mind. Harrison openly showed his distrust and continued to berate the Prophet for intriguing with the British. Harrison chose not to believe his denials. Nevertheless, he sent the Prophet back to Tippecanoe with a token gift of food and ammunition. He wrote Secretary of War Eustis that the affair was no more than the product of British intrigue in anticipation of war between Great Britain and the United States. This information was, he said, "the result of all my inquiries," [10] but it was actually little more than Harrison's obsession influencing his judgment.

Harrison's motives had been augmented by the movement toward statehood that animated the citizens of Indiana Territory. In March 1809, the Territory had been cut down, and much of the land that remained belonged to the Indians. If sufficient numbers of white men were to come into the area to achieve statehood for Indiana, it seemed to Harrison necessary that far more land be opened to settlement; the Indians owned and occupied a majority of the land in the Territory. As early as May—well in advance of the Prophet's visit—Harrison had written to Eustis to say that, in his opinion, it was time to extinguish the Indians' land titles. Eustis gave the matter some thought and agreed by midsummer. Even while Harrison was scolding the Prophet for his alleged plan to wipe out the white settlements, he was negotiating with various tribes to obtain more land.

Thus encouraged, Harrison sent messages to the Eel River, Miami and Potawatomi tribes, summoning them to a council at Fort Wayne in September. The Delaware were also invited. By the Treaty of Grouseland, the tract of land along the Wabash and White Rivers that Harrison hoped to acquire by a new treaty had been guaranteed to the sole ownership of the Miami, the Ouiatenon and the Eel River tribes. Harrison invited the Delaware and Potawatomi not so much to prevent later claims as to enlist their interest in concluding the treaty successfully for the United States. As these tribes would also receive extra annuities, they were accordingly enthusiastic for the sale of lands they did not own.

The Miami, however, were bitterly opposed to any cession of more land. The Ouiatenon and the Kickapoo, who lived on part of the land that Harrison wanted, were not present. Not a single Shawnee attended the council. Nevertheless, Harrison pressed hard for the coveted land. The Delaware and the Potawatomi were naturally eager for the sale to be accomplished; they had nothing to lose and everything to gain. Though Harrison had at first given strict orders that the whiskey brought to the council be kept locked up, he was presently persuaded that a little liquor might mellow the recalcitrant Miami. Withholding the annuities until a treaty was signed was another form of pressure that Harrison did not hesitate to apply. Even so, it was not until the end of September that the Treaty of Fort Wayne was signed; Harrison gained for the United States close to 3 million acres of land for compensation, which, as he wrote to Eustis, "is as low as could possibly be made." [11] Before the end of the year, Harrison persuaded the chiefs of the Ouiatenon and the Kickapoo to sign separate treaties of ratification.

Harrison's unseemly greed, however, had the unforeseen effect of enraging Tecumseh and the Shawnee. Tecumseh, returning from a mission to the Iroquois, was met by runners, who informed him of events at Fort Wayne. Tecumseh let it be known that he meant to kill the chiefs who had signed the treaty and particularly those who had presumed to transfer land that they did not own. His anger at Harrison and the Americans attracted a greater following than ever; by the spring of 1810, Harrison's spies at Tippecanoe reported that at least a thousand warriors had rallied behind Tecumseh. Not long after, Harrison learned that Indians of the Sauk, Fox and Winnebago tribes were coming to join the Shawnee and that efforts were being made to enlist the Choctaw and the Creek.

He wrote to the Prophet, thinking him still the principal agitator against the Americans. He sent conciliatory letters to the

Shawnee. He also sent many letters to the Secretary of War, and on one occasion Eustis suggested that "the surest means of securing the good behavior from this conspicuous personage and his brother, would be to make them prisoners." [12] Perhaps Harrison had some such plan in mind when he sent a letter by the hand of Joseph Barron, his interpreter, inviting the Prophet to lay the Shawnee complaint before him and promising, however falsely, that if the Prophet could prove that the Shawnee owned the land transferred by the Treaty of Fort Wayne, the treaty would be canceled and the land restored to the Indians.

The response to his request was considerably more impressive than Harrison had expected. Tecumseh sent word that he, accompanied by the Prophet, would come to talk with Harrison. The Governor had directed that Tecumseh should bring no more than a small party as an escort, but, as spies in Vincennes had informed Tecumseh that the territorial government had mustered two companies of militia at Vincennes, the chieftain chose three hundred warriors to accompany him. Early in August 1810, they came down the Wabash in a procession of eighty canoes and pirogues.[13]

From Fort Knox, Captain George Rogers Clark Floyd, in command, saw the Shawnee approaching Vincennes. He descended to the river's edge and ordered the procession to halt. Tecumseh, invested with dignity in his simple deerskin garb, which he wore on all occasions, signaled the approach to shore. Floyd saw that the Indians were covered with their red war paint and were fully armed, prepared for any contingency. He was impressed with Tecumseh's bearing. "A daring, bold looking fellow," he called him but "one of the finest looking men I ever saw." The Prophet, on the other hand, though splendidly clad in the trappings he assumed as a spiritual leader, made no such impression on Floyd.

Fort Knox was being improved. The violence of the Shawnee reaction to the Treaty of Fort Wayne had alarmed Harrison, who had appealed to the Secretary of War to reinforce the scant garrison at the fort. Captain Thornton Posey and his company had reached Vincennes early in July and, acting under Harrison's orders, had set about building a blockhouse and erecting a picket palisade around the fort. Floyd had come on July 31. Despite the reinforcement of the garrison, there were far from enough regulars in Fort Knox to engage three hundred picked Shawnee warriors.

Returning to the fort, Floyd watched the Indians move down river toward Vincennes. But the Shawnee did not go into the settlement; instead they went into camp not far from the river a mile above Vincennes. They were thus in a disadvantageous position if they contemplated any hostility, for they were between the regulars in Fort Knox and the militia in Vincennes. Floyd concluded, reasonably enough, that the arms the Shawnee carried were defensive. Furthermore, he had observed among them a scattering of squaws, who were not likely to be included in a war party.

On the following morning, Harrison, who had been kept informed of the Shawnee's activity, sent Joseph Barron to invite Tecumseh to a council the following day. Tecumseh, however, was not to be hurried; he returned word that he would come later and inquired whether or not armed men would be among those at council. Tecumseh was wary of any possible trap, but, if Harrison had entertained any wild hope of taking Tecumseh and the Prophet prisoners, he had quickly abandoned it on hearing of the large band of warriors accompanying the Shawnee brothers.

When at last Tecumseh, accompanied by thirty of his warriors, made his appearance at Grouseland, he saw not only members of the militia at hand but also regulars from Fort Knox. He suspected treachery and would not approach the portico of Grouseland; Harrison had to move his chair and those of his party out and away from the portico. But the first meeting was interrupted by rain just as Harrison finished outlining his hope of exploring with Tecumseh the difficulties that existed between the whites and the Indians. Though the council assembled again on the following day, it was only to hear brief speeches by both the Governor and Tecumseh, and it was not until August 20 that the council was convened again to hear Tecumseh's address.

Tecumseh opened by commanding the Governor's close attention. Tecumseh was thoroughly conversant with the history of the Indians—not only of the Shawnee, but also of all the tribes—

since the coming of the white men to North America; he knew the entire sorry history of broken treaties and promises. He had no intention of recounting that whole history but began instead by outlining the relations of the Indians with the French and the British. He spoke of the treaties made with the white men and of how they were broken. He spoke particularly of the Treaty of Greenville in 1795:

> Since the peace was made, you have killed some of the Shawnee, Winnebago, Delaware, and Miami; and you have taken our lands from us; and I do not see how we can remain at peace with you, if you continue to do so. You try to force the red people to do some injury. It is you that are pushing them on to do mischief. You endeavor to make distinctions. You wish to prevent the Indians to do as we wish them, to unite and let them consider their lands as the common property of the whole. You take tribes aside, and advise them not to come into this measure; and, until our design is accomplished, we do not wish to accept of your invitation to go and see the president. The reason, I tell you this, is, you want, by your distinctions of Indian tribes, in allotting to each a particular tract of land, to make them to war with each other. You never see an Indian come and endeavor to make the white people do so. You are continually driving the red people; when, at last, you will drive them into the great lake, where they can't either stand or work.

He recited specific grievances:

> You recall the time when the Delaware lived near the Americans, and had confidence in their promises of friendship, and thought they were secure, yet one of the Delaware towns was surprised, and the men, women and children were murdered? These same promises were given to the Shawnee. Flags were presented to my people and they were told they were now the children of the Americans. "These flags will be as security for you. If the white people intend to do you harm, hold up your flags. You will then be safe from all danger." We followed this course in good faith. But what happened? The very person bearing a flag was murdered! So were others in our village. Now, Brother, after this bitter experience, can you blame me for placing little confidence in the promises of our fathers, the Americans?

He came presently to the Treaty of Fort Wayne:

> The land that was sold, and the goods that were given for it, was done only by a few. The treaty was afterward brought here, and the Ouiatenon were induced to give their consent, because of their small numbers. . . . We are prepared to punish those chiefs who may come forward to propose to sell the land. If you continue to purchase of them, it will produce war among the different tribes and, at last, I do not know what will be the consequence to the white people. . . . Those that did sell, did not own the land. These tribes set up a claim; but the tribes with me will not agree to their claim. If the land is not restored to us, you will see, when we return to our homes, how it will be settled. We shall have a great council, at which all the tribes will be present, when we shall show to those who sold, that they had no right to the claim they set up; and we will see what will be done with those chiefs that did sell the land to you. I am not alone in this determination. It is the determination of all the warriors and red people that listen to me. I now wish you to listen to me. If you do not, it will appear as if you wished me to kill all the chiefs that sold you the land.

In his own words he confirmed the rumors that had reached Harrison's ears, and he directed particular abuse at the Potawatomi chief, Winamac, who was Harrison's friend and sat nearby, calling him a black dog and a liar who sowed dissension between white men and red. His address was lengthy and eloquent and occasionally poured forth so passionately that Harrison's interpreter could not follow it.

> It is true I am a Shawnee. My forefathers were warriors. Their son is a warrior. From them I take only my existence. From my tribe I take nothing. I am the maker of my own fortune. And oh, that I might make the fortunes of my red people, and of my country, as great as the conceptions of my mind, when I think of the Great Spirit that rules this universe! I would not then come to Governor Harrison and ask him to tear up the treaty and obliterate the landmarks; but I would say to him, "Sir, you have permission to return to your own country." The being within me, communing with past ages, tells me that once, and until lately, there were no white men at all on this island; that it then

belonged to the red men, children of the same parents, placed
on it by the Great Spirit that made them, to keep it, to traverse
it, to enjoy its productions and to fill it with the same race. Once
they were a happy race. Now they are made miserable by the
white people who are never contented but always encroaching.

The way, the only way, to check and to stop this evil is for
all the red men to unite in claiming a common and equal right
in the land. That is how it was at first and should be still, for the
land never was divided but belongs to all, for the use of every
one. No groups among us have a right to sell, even to one another,
much less to strangers who want all and will not do with less.

He made sport of the white men's greed for land: "Sell a
country! Why not sell the air, the clouds and the great sea, as
well as the earth?" He scored the white man for his past: "How
can we have confidence in the white people? When Jesus Christ
came upon the earth, you killed Him, and nailed Him to a cross.
You thought He was dead, but you were mistaken." He said that
the Indians were about accomplishing no more than their white
brethren: "The States have set the example of forming a union
among all the fires—why should they censure the Indians for
following it?" [14]

The speech was a remarkable document, passionately delivered.
Toward its end, Tecumseh put Harrison on the defensive by demanding a statement of the Governor's intentions about rescind-
ing the Treaty of Fort Wayne. To Harrison, of course, this remarkable address seemed pretentious and arrogant; it was impossible for Harrison, the Virginia patrician, to look upon an
uneducated Indian as his equal, though he was now aware that
Tecumseh considered himself so. He was not able to reply at
once; he had not anticipated the burden of Tecumseh's address,
not being accustomed to any dealing with an Indian of Tecumseh's prestige and dignity.

When at last Harrison rose and began his reply to Tecumseh,
he launched into the feeble charge that the Shawnee, being originally from Georgia, had no right to land that had always belonged to the Miami, though Tecumseh had laid claim to the
land as an Indian, not as a Shawnee. Tecumseh listened impas-
sively. Harrison droned on for a quarter of an hour more and then

made a statement that aroused Tecumseh to fury. Speaking of the compensation paid to the Indians for their land, he set forth a claim that he knew to be a falsehood: that the United States had been fair in dealing with the Indians.

As soon as the interpreter had given Harrison's statement in Shawnee, Tecumseh leapt to his feet, shouting angrily: "It is false! He lies!" He began to abuse Harrison. The council was disrupted at once. John Gibson, Secretary of Indiana Territory, sitting at Harrison's side, ordered Lieutenant Jesse Jennings from Fort Knox to bring up the guard of twelve riflemen standing by not far away. Captain Floyd produced a side arm, while Tecumseh's warriors came to their feet behind him and drew their tomahawks in readiness. For some tense moments hostilities appeared to be imminent. Then Governor Harrison, understanding at last that he had been insulted, adjourned the council, turned and went into his home, with his guests following him.

Tecumseh and his warriors returned to the Shawnee camp. By morning his anger had cooled, and he sent his apologies to Harrison with Joseph Barron. Harrison magnanimously came to visit Tecumseh in the Shawnee camp, where Tecumseh, now in good humor, edged him to the very end of a bench on which both were sitting and drew the parallel between his action and the design of the Americans in pushing the Indians off the land. He made clear his defensive motive when he told Harrison he was only attempting to construct a dam against the intentions of the Americans.

On August 22 the council was convened once again. On this occasion, Tecumseh did recite the long list of Indian grievances against the white men, beginning with the time of the first landing but reciting in particular detail from the period of the Revolutionary War. In writing to the Secretary of War later, Harrison said of these grievances "There are unfortunately too many of them," though he accused Tecumseh of exaggerating them. Harrison, in turn, wanted some assurance from Tecumseh that the Shawnee and their allies would not hamper or prevent the surveying of the land obtained by the recent treaties; Tecumseh would not give him such assurance, saying that the Indians wanted the land for themselves and expected the whites to maintain the present boundary line, by which he meant the boundary set prior to the Treaty of Fort Wayne.

Tecumseh and his warriors and squaws returned up the Wabash, and Harrison wrote reports to Washington of the speeches the Shawnee leader had given. The speech had alarmed him and all who heard it and subsequently learned of it. The threatening nature of Tecumseh's speech was bound to inhibit settlement of the territory. With approximately 25,000 free white residents by 1810, Indiana Territory was moving steadily toward statehood, and Harrison feared that Tecumseh's intransigence would delay the growth of the territory. His fears impressed Washington and persuaded the Secretary of War to order more regulars into the area; early in October, 120 men under Captain Joseph Cross arrived at the garrison at Fort Knox, though there was not room enough for them in the fort itself, insufficient barracks having been constructed, and the force had to go into camp near the fort. Governor Harrison was informed by Eustis that a new fort might be put up farther north along the Wabash and that both Posey's and Cross' detachments should be quartered in or near Vincennes pending further orders.

Following the council at Grouseland, Harrison was fully aware that Tecumseh was the most dangerous Indian in the Territory, and he was determined to seize upon any good excuse to engage the Indians under Tecumseh's leadership. There was no lack of incidents, but the depredations of the Indians were balanced by white outrages against the red men. Attempts to bring the murderers of Indians to justice were usually thwarted; when Laurent Bazadone, an innkeeper at Vincennes, shot an unarmed Muskogee, the jury at a trial ordered by Harrison speedily acquitted Bazadone, without regard for the effect such action would have among the Indians, whose determination to resist the Americans was thereby hardened.

Harrison meant to press a campaign against the Shawnee. He requisitioned arms early in 1811, asking for five hundred rifles. He wrote to the Secretary of War that the Prophet and his followers intended to advance upon the settlements, particularly Vincennes; this threat was wholly a figment of his imagination, for the Prophet was living quietly with his followers in the Indians' territory. By summer, too, the troops at Fort Knox were becoming restive. Captain Posey, then in command, shot and killed Lieutenant Jesse Jennings because of personal differences. The murder took place on June 23, and Posey escaped from detention. As Posey was at that time in command of Fort Knox, he left the fort without a leader. He was succeeded by Zachary Taylor, who remained in charge of the regulars long enough in the summer of 1811 to improve thoroughly the defenses of Fort Knox.

Harrison presently found a reason to threaten the Shawnee. An increasing number of hostile acts culminated in the murder of four white men by two Potawatomi on the Missouri River. Though the murderers fled to the protection of a Potawatomi chief, Harrison chose to believe that they were with the Prophet and sent him a demand that the murderers be surrendered for trial. It was not the Prophet but Tecumseh who answered, telling Harrison bluntly that not only were the two Potawatomi not with the Shawnee but also that they would not be surrendered if they were. He referred pointedly to the "justice" meted out to the Vincennes murderer of the Muskogee. Harrison was left seething.

Not long after, the Prophet seized a salt cargo passing Tippecanoe. Harrison promptly sent a threatening speech through Captain Walter Gibson, informing the Prophet and Tecumseh that many men would come to punish them. Tecumseh sent word to the Governor that he would call on him in Vincennes in eighteen days, and once again Harrison—possibly still dreaming of capturing Tecumseh and the Prophet—adjured him to bring no more than thirty men as escort.

Once more Tecumseh and the Prophet came with hundreds of warriors and squaws, and Tecumseh presented himself at the council with Harrison accompanied by no less than 175 fully armed warriors, for Harrison obviously had a large armed escort of his own. Harrison was in a truculent mood; he did not intend to be insulted and embarrassed again. He announced at once that he would not discuss the land bought at the Treaty of Fort Wayne; this matter was in the hands of the President, and Tecumseh would have to discuss it in Washington. In any case, Harrison was not interested in peace; he had made up his mind to move against the Prophet's town, with or without reason, and nothing Tecumseh might say could alter his decision.

Tecumseh, however, did not trust Harrison any more than he had ever trusted him. His answers to Harrison's demands were circumlocutory and evasive. He affected to be puzzled by Harrison's concern about the salt that the Prophet had seized, pointing out that, when, the year before, the Prophet had declined to accept salt, the Governor had been angry; now that he had taken it, Harrison was equally angry. It seemed to Tecumseh, as he put it, contradictory. As for the two Potawatomi murderers, they were not with the Shawnee.

Tecumseh once more claimed the right of the Indians to band themselves together in a confederation, just as the whites had done with their states. Indeed, he was currently on the way to visit the southern tribes to enlist them, too, in the confederation. He was clearly not contemplating any aggressive action, and, to emphasize the fact, he promised to send runners throughout the tribes allied to the confederacy commanding that no hostile act against the whites should be committed while he was gone. At the same time, he suggested that the white settlers refrain from coming into the disputed territory.

Harrison made no promises. As the council continued into the night, he grew more blunt. Pointing to the moon, he told Tecumseh that the moon would fall before the President would permit his children to be murdered without punishment. Nor, he went on, would the President give up the land that he had "fairly acquired from its rightful owners." With this blatant falsehood, he adjourned the council.

The Indians remained at Vincennes for a few days. Then the Prophet led the majority of them back up the Wabash, while Tecumseh, with two dozen warriors, went down the river, well aware that his final words to Harrison were prophetic:

> As the great chief over the mountains is to decide the matter, I hope the Great Spirit will put sense enough in his head to order you to give up those lands. It is true, he may sit in his fine house and drink his wine, while you and I have to fight it out.[15]

Tecumseh was still far from his initial destination—the Chickasaw—when Harrison began preparing for his march upon Tippecanoe. He sent to Kentucky for volunteers. By the end of
September a thousand men were assembling at Vincennes. They
included the Fourth U.S. Regiment from Kentucky, under the
command of Colonel John P. Boyd, as well as Captain Posey's
company from Fort Knox. The fort would remain garrisoned by
only a skeleton force under the command of Lieutenant Josiah
Bacon, who, having been injured in a powder explosion, was unable to make the journey north. Bacon and his wife moved into
the fort.

Though permission for the expedition had come from the Secretary of War, Eustis cautioned Harrison to avoid battle if at all
possible; it would be preferable to scatter the followers without
bloodshed. At all costs Harrison was to avoid any conflict with
the British, for Eustis had been impressed by the obsessiveness of
Harrison's conviction that the British were inciting the Indians.

On September 26, Harrison and his army set out from Vincennes. Harrison's force consisted of territorial militia, Kentucky
volunteers and the regulars commanded by Colonel Boyd. This
force moved up along the Wabash into the area transferred by
the Treaty of Fort Wayne, halting on October 1 at the high
ground the French knew as "Terre Haute." There the army encamped and immediately began to construct a fort, which, because Harrison had for so long advocated it, was named "Fort
Harrison."

While the fort was under construction, Harrison sent representations to the Prophet in the persons of some of the Delaware
chiefs in an effort to persuade him to move. This effort was his
concession to the Secretary of War's request that he attempt to
avoid bloodshed. He very probably foresaw that the attempt
would come to nothing; his envoys were treated badly and sent
back by the Prophet, which Harrison duly reported to Eustis:
"Nothing now remains but to chastise him and he shall certainly
get it." Harrison was obviously looking forward to battle. "I
promise you Sir that all the objects intended by the Expedition
shall be effected." [16]

It was nearing the end of October. Fort Harrison was complete, and the army was free to move. The force reached a spot two miles from the Prophet's town in the evening of November 6. There they were met by messengers from the Prophet, who proposed a conference, to be held next day. Harrison was amenable. The site of the conference with the Prophet's messengers was not, however, suitable for a camping ground, and Harrison asked the Indians to designate a better site. The Indians indicated an anvil-shaped area of high ground along Burnett's Creek, a tributary to the Wabash, not far west of the Prophet's town at the junction of the Tippecanoe and the Wabash. The site was the best available; woods to the left and rear of it gave Harrison's men protection, though they also made it possible for any enemy to approach under cover.

Harrison expected no attack. Nevertheless, he laid out his camp in the shape of a triangle, suiting it to the terrain and dispersing the regulars along the sides of the triangle, together with units of the militia. He instructed his men to sleep with their guns ready to hand. While the expedition prepared for the night, the Indians at the Prophet's town were prevailing upon the Prophet, who was trying to follow Tecumseh's instructions to avoid battle, to attack the whites. After some attempts to counsel peace, the Prophet gave in, and, as the night wore on, the Indian warriors went into position for battle, intending to rush the camp and, if possible, to kill Harrison or take him prisoner while the invading army was in disorder.

The Indian attack commenced before dawn immediately before the sounding of reveille. A sentinel's shot gave warning of the attack, which followed hard upon it. It was a fierce engagement; though the Americans were briefly at a disadvantage in their surprise and the Indians broke through the lines here and there to reach the tents, the confusion was quickly overcome. The battle lasted two hours; with daylight, the Indians withdrew, having lost approximately forty braves compared to Harrison's loss of 61 men and 127 wounded. The Indians' wounded were quickly carried away.

Harrison later gave this account of the battle to Secretary of War Eustis:

I had risen at a quarter after four o'clock, and the signal for
calling out the men would have been given in two minutes, when
the attack commenced. It began on the left flank; but a single
gun was fired by the sentinels, or by the guard in that direction,
which made not the least resistance, but abandoned their officer
and fled into camp; and the first notice which the troops of that
flank had of their danger, was from the yells of the savages
within a short distance of the line; but, even under these circumstances, the men were not wanting to themselves or to the occasion. Such of them as were awake, or were easily awakened,
seized their arms, and took their stations; others, which were
more tardy, had to contend with the enemy in the doors of their
tents. The storm first fell upon Captain Barton's company of the
4th United States regiment, and Captain Guiger's company of
mounted riflemen, which formed the left angle of the rear line.
... Our fires afforded a partial light, which, if it gave us some
opportunity of taking our position, was still more advantageous
to the enemy—affording them the means of taking a surer aim.
They were, therefore, extinguished as soon as possible....

In the course of a few minutes after the commencement of the
attack, the fire extended along the left flank, the whole of the
front, the right flank, and part of the rear line. Upon Spencer's
mounted riflemen, and the right of Warrick's company, which
was posted on the right of the rear line, it was excessively severe.
Captain Spencer, and his first and second lieutenants, were killed;
and Captain Warrick mortally wounded.... My great object was
to keep the lines entire—to prevent the enemy from breaking
into the camp, until daylight should enable me to make a general
and effectual charge. With this view I had reinforced every part
of the line that had suffered much; and as soon as the approach
of morning discovered itself, I withdrew from the front line
Snelling's Posey's (under Lieutenant Albright) and Scott's; and
from the rear line, Wilson's companies, and drew them up upon
the left flank; and at the same time, I ordered Cook's and Baen's
companies—the former from the rear, and the latter from the
front line—to reinforce the right flank; foreseeing that, at these
points, the enemy would make their last efforts.... The Indians
were driven by the infantry at the point of the bayonet; and the
dragoons pursued and forced them into a marsh, where they
could not be followed. Captain Cook and Lieutenant Larrabee
had, agreeably to my order, marched their companies to the

right flank, and formed them under the fire of the enemy; and being then joined by the riflemen of that flank, had charged the Indians, killing a number, and put the rest to precipitate flight....

The whole of the infantry formed a small brigade, under the immediate orders of Colonel Boyd. The colonel, throughout the action, manifested equal zeal and bravery in carrying into execution my orders—in keeping the men to their posts, and exhorting them to fight with valor. His brigade-major, Clarke, and his aid-de-camp, George Croghan, esq., were also very serviceably employed.... Major G. R. C. Floyd, the senior officer of the 4th United States regiment, commanded immediately the battalion of that regiment, which was in the front line. His conduct, during the action, was entirely to my satisfaction....[17]

After the battle, Harrison ordered some earthworks thrown up. On the next day, November 8, the expedition marched upon the Prophet's town. The Americans found it deserted, confiscated some of the provisions and destroyed the remainder, together with the town. On November 9, the expedition broke camp and began the march back to Vincennes, much encumbered with its wounded. The men reached Vincennes nine days later, and their account of the battle spread jubilation among the citizens of that village, as well as all along the frontier.

2

The battle of Tippecanoe, which Harrison defended and vaunted at such length for years afterward and which was, in fact, to lead him to the Presidency of the United States, was a venture wholly on the debit side of the ledger. It accomplished nothing for the United States; indeed, it so worsened the relations between the Americans and the Indians as to persuade a large number of the tribes under the leadership of Tecumseh to throw in their fortunes with the British. As this result was not immediately apparent, however, Harrison's expedition was much approved throughout the territory.

By spring of 1812, the Prophet and his followers were back at the site of the town on the Tippecanoe. Throughout that spring, while the Americans were engaged in vilifying the British in

Canada in preparation for an open break, Indian depredations increased. Tecumseh restrained the warriors from open warfare, but he could do nothing to prevent isolated murders and raids. Nor could he do anything to incite the British, who continued to do all in their power to dissuade the Indians from conflict with the Americans.

By June, the war party in Congress won the day. On June 18, war was declared upon Great Britain. Command of the army on the frontier was given to an ex-Revolutionary officer, General William Hull, Governor of Michigan Territory and an inept, timid and sadly impulsive man, who was instructed to fortify Detroit. With the coming of the war, Tecumseh not unexpectedly led more than a thousand warriors to join the British. They were presently augmented by other bands, some from as far away as the west shore of the Mississippi, from which the Sauk chief, Black Hawk, led a force to serve under Tecumseh.

The Indians augmented the inferior Canadian forces and contributed notably to the early British successes in the War of 1812. By September Mackinac, Fort Dearborn and Detroit had all fallen to the British. Detroit, with its superior forces, fell largely through the timidity and apprehension of General Hull, who surrendered it without a battle.

These events, following closely one upon another, alarmed Vincennes, in common with other settlements in the territory. Fear of the Indians was now intensified, and the citizens of Vincennes, who had once rejoiced at the moving of the fort to the heights three miles north of the town, began to realize that Fort Knox at Petit Rocher afforded little protection to Vincennes.

There was, however, no scarcity of armed men in and near Vincennes. Colonel William Russell, commanding a company of regular infantry and one of Rangers—to whom the protection of Indiana Territory had largely fallen, as the regulars were required to garrison the forts—came through on his way to join Governor Ninian Edwards of Illinois Territory. Russell's arrival coincided with news from the north that Fort Harrison was under Indian attack; he therefore diverted his course to lend his aid to Zachary Taylor, in command at Fort Harrison. Then he went on to join Edwards.

In late September, Major General Samuel Hopkins came to Vincennes with two thousand men, under orders to drive the Indians out of the Wabash and Illinois River valleys. The alarmed citizenry of both Indiana and Illinois Territories had taken to throwing up forts and blockhouses in some profusion following news of the American defeats to the north, and Indian attacks on Forts Wayne and Harrison persuaded all the settlers to the south that the Indians intended a large-scale invasion of those settled areas.

But the Indians inimical to the settlers were farther to the north with the British, and General Hopkins's expedition accomplished little. The guides frequently lost their way, the supplies ran low and the troops—disregarding specific orders—destroyed some Indian villages, chiefly those of Indians friendly to the Americans. They met with no opposition, as many of the towns—including the Prophet's town—had been evacuated. At the site of the battle of Tippecanoe, they found that the bodies of the Americans slain in that engagement had been dug up by the Indians and scalped; they paused to rebury them. Snow and bitter weather forced them back upon Fort Harrison and from there to Vincennes, leaving behind them as many angry settlers, whose farms had been pillaged by the hungry soldiers, as Indians. Another expedition under General Samuel Tupper of the Ohio militia, ordered by Harrison to the Miami Rapids to destroy any crops in that area, failed even more ignominiously, for Tupper's men refused to go as far as the rapids. Similar expeditions were no more successful.

Nevertheless, despite the evidence of the Hopkins expedition that unfriendly Indians were many miles away from Vincennes, the citizenry clamored for the relocation of Fort Knox. They wanted the fort closer to the village, so that it could be used in the village's defense. Harrison may have relayed the request of the citizens of Vincennes to the Secretary of War, but he was now more often away from Grouseland than at home; he was in Cincinnati, in Louisville, wherever, in fact, he saw any possible advantage in furthering his goal, which was the command of an army to recapture Detroit. He had been stung by some of the criticisms of the campaign that led to the battle of Tippecanoe, and he hoped to redeem his image as a war hero by retaking Detroit.

On February 27, 1813, President Madison nominated Senator Thomas Posey for Governor of Indiana Territory; the nomination was confirmed on March 3, and, at the same time, Harrison was raised to the rank of major general and given command of the Eighth Military District, which included Ohio, Kentucky and the territories of Indiana, Michigan, Illinois and Missouri. This command involved not only the retaking of Detroit and the invasion of Canada but also the defense of many miles of frontier. While Posey settled his affairs prior to coming to Vincennes late in May, Secretary of the Territory John Gibson served as Acting Governor.

Sometime in the course of that winter, the order came through from Washington for the relocation of Fort Knox, for on March 10, 1813, Acting Governor Gibson reported to Secretary of War William Armstrong that much of the needed timber had been brought down the Wabash for the new fort, as authorized by Armstrong's predecessor, Eustis. In the course of this month also, the garrison from Fort Knox was quartered in Vincennes while the new Fort Knox was being built on the site selected for it; the timber brought down the river came from the dismantled fort on Petit Rocher.

The third Fort Knox rose on the site of old Fort Sackville. There was some disagreement about the site among the officers. The construction was in charge of Lieutenant Thomas H. Richardson, who had a hundred soldiers at work on the fort. There was some complaint, reminiscent of previous complaints about the garrison, that some of the regulars were spending more time in the taverns than about their duties.[18]

In April of that year, Zachary Taylor came to Vincennes again, this time to recruit men. He was not enthusiastic about his task, for the number of inhabitants at Vincennes had declined, and he could not compete with the Rangers, who received $30 a month against the $8 offered to the regulars. Not long after this effort, Taylor was named to command the garrison at the new Fort Knox. He elected not to live within the fortification but chose instead to live in a small house owned by Judge Benjamin Parke in Vincennes.

His command was a relatively quiet one. Not only were the Indians passive during the remainder of 1813, but also the Indiana Rangers were now entrusted with the task of pacifying them, and the regulars were seldom called upon. Such Indian action as took place in the general vicinity of Vincennes was minor. On one occasion, Colonel William Russell of the Seventh United States Regiment ordered the Rangers to clear the country between Vincennes and the mouth of the White River of Indians reported seen there. On another, three stolen horses, abandoned by Indians aware of pursuit, were recovered. On yet another, a small band of Indians was vigorously pursued and one of them killed while the others fled. These incidents did not involve Fort Knox or its garrison.

In the course of 1813, Governor Posey moved the capital of the Territory from Vincennes to Corydon, greatly diminishing the bustle that had been maintained at Vincennes during Harrison's term of office. Harrison was engaging the British and the Indians with such success that the British were forced to retreat from Detroit and Malden; they were finally defeated in the decisive battle of the Thames early in October, a battle in the course of which Tecumseh was killed.

Vincennes was well removed from the scenes of conflict. Indeed, Vincennes was no longer on the western frontier, which had moved to the Mississippi. Following the battle of the Thames, most of Indiana Territory entered upon a period of calm; fear of the Indians diminished, and throughout 1814 there was scarcely an Indian incident to be recorded. By the time that Zachary Taylor was replaced as commander of Fort Knox by Brevet Major John T. Chunn, it was evident that the usefulness of Fort Knox would soon be over.

It was finally Judge Benjamin Parke who suggested that Fort Knox be abandoned; he wrote to Governor Posey on May 10, 1815, pointing out that the garrison at Fort Harrison should be adequate for the protection of the lower Wabash valley and the settlements on both sides of the river. The decision took some time —almost a year, in fact—but by 1816 the abandonment of Fort

Knox was decided upon. The Vincennes *Western Sun* from January 6 to February 10 of that year carried advertisements requesting the holders of public arms to surrender them to Brevet Major Chunn for shipment to Newport, Kentucky.

By February 10 the garrison of Fort Knox had gone to Fort Harrison, and the fort itself stood deserted, a symbol of the westward movement of the American frontier. It was not left standing long.

Epilogue

❧

Clark's services during the Revolution were of incalculable value, amid difficulties only too easy calculable. It is probably true that he added three—perhaps five—states to the Union. He is one of the few soldiers in American military history—or any other history—who were never once defeated and never once surprised.

—John Bakeless,
Background to Glory

❧

George Rogers Clark never received his back pay. Neither Virginia nor the Congress of the United States ever acknowledged the debts that he had incurred in the service of his country, though Virginia voted him a trifling pension in his last years and a sword when he could no longer wield it. His property was stripped from him by creditors, who turned upon him when Virginia and the Congress refused to honor the orders for supplies that Clark had signed. Not for over a century and a half did the nation acknowledge its incalculable debt of gratitude to George Rogers Clark.

Then the State of Indiana, together with Knox County and the City of Vincennes, purchased the site of old Fort Sackville and land around it for the construction of a suitable memorial to Clark. The United States Government appropriated more than $1.5 million to erect the memorial and improve the grounds around it. The memorial is a circular Doric temple, easily one of the most attractive memorials in the country. It was dedicated June 14, 1936, by President Franklin Delano Roosevelt.

"Events of history," he said, "take on their due proportions when viewed in the light of time. With every passing year, the capture of Vincennes, more than a century and a half ago when the thirteen Colonies were seeking their independence, assumes greater and more permanent significance.... In the year 1778 the picture of this Western country was dark indeed. The English held all the region northwest of the Ohio, and their Indian allies were burning cabins and driving fleeing families back across the mountains south of the river. Three regular forts were all that remained in Kentucky, and their fall seemed inevitable. Then, against this dark background, stood forth the tall young Virginian, George Rogers Clark. Out of despair and destruction he brought concerted action. With a flash of genius the twenty-six-year-old leader conceived a campaign that was a brilliant masterpiece of military strategy."

The slightly larger-than-life-size bronze statue of George Rogers Clark that stands under the dome of the memorial dominates it. Created by Hermon A. MacNeil, it is mounted on mottled Italian marble, facing the entrance and central to seven large oil paintings on Belgian linen, each 16 by 28 feet, the work of Ezra Winter, which are affixed to the circular wall all around the statue. These somewhat glamorized paintings—Clark's men, for instance, were in fact considerably more rough and ragged than the artist has depicted them—constitute a sequence of scenes that tell the story of Clark's heroic venture and its significance to the country.

They begin with a view of Clark and fellow pioneers entering Kentucky and continue with paintings showing Clark at Cahokia, offering the Indians the choice of peace or war; Clark and his army fording the icy Wabash bent upon surprising the British in Fort Sackville; Clark and his ragged army beginning the attack on the fort at Vincennes; Hamilton surrendering Fort Sackville to Clark; the reading of the ordinance of 1787, establishing a government for the Northwest Territory, at Marietta; and the lowering of the French flag at St. Louis, signifying the Louisiana Purchase of 1803 and the westward movement of America. The seating encircling the interior of the memorial below the paintings is of French marble, and the floor is of Tennessee marble; the exterior wainscoting is in two colors of Minnesota granite.

Not far from the impressive memorial, which commands the eye for some distance, on the eastern edge of the handsomely landscaped grounds, another statue, sculptured by John Sigel, looks toward the memorial and Vincennes. It is, fittingly, that of Francis Vigo, seated and with head slightly turned, as if he were gazing toward the great land that his unceasing assistance to George Rogers Clark helped to secure for the country that Vigo adopted and loved.

On August 20, 1940, the Clark Memorial was transferred to the control of the Indiana Department of Conservation, which has maintained it in its Division of State Parks since then. Many thousands of visitors stop at the Memorial every year, far more sensible of Clark's great contribution to the growth and security of the United States than were the government and the citizens of his own time.

Notes

I. The Sieur de Vincennes Builds a Fort

[1] This error of identification has been responsible for a persisting belief that the post at Vincennes was established in 1702. As recently as 1965, no less distinguished an historian than Samuel Eliot Morison wrote in his *Oxford History of the American People* that Vincennes was established as a trading post "within a year" of 1699. His reference could only have been to the Cairo post founded by Juchereau and abandoned three years later following Juchereau's death of yellow fever.

[2] The post at Vincennes was known as "Little Ouiatenon," abbreviated on English maps of the period as "L. Wiaut." After the death of the Sieur de Vincennes in 1736, it was called "Post St. Ange"—or, by the English, "Fort St. Anne." But it was most commonly called simply "the post" or "Opost" on the lower Wabash and did not take the name "Vincennes" until the middle of the eighteenth century, according to Jacob Piatt Dunn in *The Mission to the Ouabache.*

[3] Pierre-Georges Roy, *Sieur de Vincennes Identified,* as quoted in Jacob Piatt Dunn, *The Mission to the Ouabache.*

[4] *Archives Nationales, Colonies.* C13 A20 246. Vincennes to Bienville, April 22, 1735.

[5] Jacob Piatt Dunn, *op. cit.*

[6] *Ibid.*

[7] Joseph Henry VanderBurgh Somes, *Old Vincennes.*

[8] *Archives Nationales, Colonies,* C13 C1, 109, as quoted in Paul C. Phillips, "Vincennes in Its Relation to French Colonial Policy," *Indiana Magazine of History,* Vol. XVII, No. 4 (December 1921).

II. George Rogers Clark

[1] Joseph Henry VanderBurgh Somes, *Old Vincennes.*

[2] Baynton, Wharton & Morgan Company of Philadelphia. George Croghan, then British Assistant Superintendent of Indian Affairs in charge of the fur country, had ambitiously persuaded this Company to invest in fur stores in Kaskaskia, Cahokia and Vincennes. Croghan overestimated the quantities furs to be had in the area, and both he and the Company failed to realize their expectations.

[3] *Illinois Historical Collections,* XI.

[4] John B. Dillon, *History of Indiana from Its Earliest Exploration by Europeans to the Close of the Territorial Government, in 1816,* as quoted in Florence Goold Watts, "Some Vincennes Documents," *Indiana Magazine of History,* Vol. 34.

[5] Florence Goold Watts, *op. cit.* This document was published in English for the first time, as translated and edited by Florence Goold Watts. The originals are to be found in the William L. Clements Library at Ann Arbor, Michigan.

[6] George Rogers Clark, *Campaign in the Illinois in 1778–9.*

[7] *Ibid.*

[8] *Ibid.* Immediately subsequent quotations are also from this source.

[9] John D. Barnhart, ed., "Lieutenant Governor Henry Hamilton's Apologia," *Indiana Magazine of History,* Vol. 52. In his excellent biography of Clark, John Bakeless writes that Hamilton "did not wait until approval came from Quebec. That would have taken weeks." One is inclined to believe that Hamilton's memory failed him.

[10] *Ibid.* Hamilton's report of September 30, 1778, gives slightly different figures, but the difference is negligible. The information in the letter to Lord Shelburne would seem to have been written from memory.

[11] *Ibid.* The settlement to which Hamilton makes reference here was the beginning of Louisville, Kentucky.

[12] *Illinois Historical Collections,* I, 226.

[13] George Rogers Clark, *Campaign in the Illinois in 1778–9.* Clark's bad spelling was often particularly far from the mark when it came to proper names. His "Mr. Vague" was, of course, Francis Vigo.

[14] *Ibid.*

[15] *Ibid.*

[16] "Major Bowman's Journal," *ibid.*

[17] Clark, *op. cit.,*

[18] *Ibid.*

[19] "Major Bowman's Journal," *ibid.*

[20] *Ibid.*

[21] *Ibid.*

[22] Barnhart, *op. cit.*

[23] "Major Bowman's Journal," in Clark, *op. cit.*

III. The Long Knives Against the Indians

[1] George Rogers Clark, *Campaign in the Illinois in 1778–9.*

[2] Clarence Walworth Alvord, ed., *Collections of the Illinois State Historical Society,* Vol. VIII.

[3] *Ibid.*

[4] *Ibid.*

[5] *Ibid.*

[6] *Ibid.*

[7] *Ibid.*

[8] *Ibid.*

[9] *Ibid.*

[10] *Ibid.* Clark's account was published in *The Maryland Journal*, October 17, 1780, and the present transcription is by Dr. Lyman Draper. It is evident that someone improved on the original.

[11] *Ibid.*

[12] *Ibid.*

[13] *Ibid.*

[14] *Ibid.*

[15] *Ibid.* The translation of the original French is by James Alton James, editor of the *George Rogers Clark Papers*.

[16] *Ibid.*

[17] *Ibid.*

IV. Major Hamtramck Takes Control

[1] Gayle Thornbrough, ed., *Outpost on the Wabash 1787–1791*.

[2] *Ibid.*

[3] *Ibid.*

[4] *Ibid.*

[5] *Ibid.*

[6] *Ibid.*

[7] *Ibid.*

[8] *Ibid.*

[9] *Ibid.*

10 *Ibid.*

11 *Ibid.*

12 *Ibid.*

13 *Ibid.*

14 *Ibid.*

15 *Ibid.*

16 *Ibid.*

17 *Ibid.*

18 *Ibid.*

19 *Ibid.*

20 *Ibid.*

21 *Ibid.*

22 *Ibid.*

23 *Ibid.*

24 Logan Esarey, *A History of Indiana from Its Exploration to 1850.*

25 Gayle Thornbrough, ed., *Outpost on the Wabash 1787–1791.*

26 *Ibid.*

27 *Ibid.*

V. The Last Years

1 Milo M. Quaife, ed., "Fort Knox Orderly Book, 1793–97," *Indiana Magazine of History,* Vol. XXXII.

2 Logan Esarey, ed., *Messages and Letters of William Henry Harrison.*

[3] *Ibid.*

[4] Clarence Edward Carter, ed., *The Territorial Papers of the United States,* Vol. VII.

[5] Esarey, *op. cit.*

[6] This treaty was repeatedly cited as one of the principal reasons for the Black Hawk War of 1832; Black Hawk claimed that he had not signed it, or that, if he had, he had not realized that he was signing away even the land on which his village stood.

[7] Florence Goold Watts, "Fort Knox: Frontier Outpost on the Wabash 1787–1816," *Indiana Magazine of History,* Vol. 62.

[8] A sketch of the Prophet reproduced in John B. Dillon, *A History of Indiana from Its Earliest Exploration by Europeans to the Close of the Territorial Government in 1816,* shows him as one-eyed and wearing a feathered turban. This sketch may have been made in his later, more peaceful years, after he had gone to live among the British.

[9] Esarey, *op. cit.*

[10] *Ibid.*

[11] *Ibid.*

[12] *Ibid.*

[13] Glenn Tucker, *Tecumseh: Vision of Glory.*

[14] Tecumseh's address is quoted in part from Tucker, *op. cit.,* and in part from Dillon, *op. cit.*

[15] Tucker, *op. cit.*

[16] Esarey, *op. cit.*

[17] *Ibid.*

[18] In her admirably succinct account of Fort Knox, Mrs. Florence Goold Watts (*op. cit.*) points out that the exact location of the third and last Fort Knox was unknown until 1956, when a letter signed by Andrew Dunn, sent from Bruceville, Indiana, on December 12, 1878, fixed the site. Dunn wrote

of the fort: "I think the fort was about five rods wide and ten rods long. It was built of hughed [*sic*] logs for pickets set in the ground and 12 or 15 feet high. There was a gate in the uper [*sic*] end of the fort and I think there was one in the lower end—there was gates in the sides." He wrote also that the third Fort Knox was torn down "some time between 1816 and 1820."

Bibliography

❧

Alvord, Clarence Walworth. *The Illinois Country, 1673–1818.* Springfield, Ill.: 1920.

———, ed. *Kaskaskia Records, 1778–1790.* Springfield, Ill.: The Trustees of the Illinois State Historical Library, 1909.

American State Papers. *Indian Affairs.* Washington, D.C.: Library of Congress.

———. *Military Affairs.* Washington, D.C.: Library of Congress.

Bakeless, John. *Background to Glory: The Life of George Rogers Clark.* Philadelphia: J. B. Lippincott Company, 1957.

Barnhart, John D., ed. *Henry Hamilton and George Rogers Clark in the American Revolution.* Crawfordsville, Ind.: R. E. Banta, 1951.

———. "Lieutenant Governor Henry Hamilton's Apologia," *Indiana Magazine of History,* Vol. 52.

Billington, Ray Allen. *Westward Expansion: A History of the American Frontier.* New York: The Macmillan Company, 1949.

Blair, Emma Helen, ed. *Indian Tribes of the Upper Mississippi Valley and Region of the Great Lakes.* Cleveland: The Arthur H. Clark Company, 1911–1912.

Blanchard, Rufus. *The Discovery and Conquests of the Northwest.* Chicago: Cushing, Thomas & Company, 1880.

Burns, Lee. *Life in Old Vincennes.* Indianapolis, Ind.: Indiana Historical Society Publications, 1929.

Carter, Clarence Edward, ed. *The Territorial Papers of the United States.* Washington: U.S. Government Printing Office, 1934 *et seq.*

Cauthorn, Henry S. *A History of the City of Vincennes.* Terre Haute: 1902.

Clark, George Rogers. *Campaign in the Illinois in 1778–9.* Cincinnati: Robert Clarke & Company, 1869.

Cleaves, Freeman. *Old Tippecanoe: William Henry Harrison and His Time.* New York: Charles Scribner's Sons, 1939.

DeHart, R. P. *Past and Present of Tippecanoe County, Indiana.* Indianapolis, Ind.: B. F. Bowen & Company, 1909.

Dillon, John B. *A History of Indiana from Its Earliest Exploration by Europeans to the Close of the Territorial Government in 1816.* Indianapolis, Ind.: Bingham & Doughty, 1859.

Draper, Lyman C. Manuscript Collection. Madison, Wis.: State Historical Society of Wisconsin.

Dunn, Jacob Piatt. *Father Gibault: The Patriot Priest of the Northwest.* Springfield, Ill.: Illinois Historical Collections.

——. *Indiana and Indianans.* New York: The American Historical Society, 1916.

——. *The Mission to the Oubache.* Indianapolis, Ind.: The Bowen-Merrill Company, 1902.

Esarey, Logan. *A History of Indiana from Its Exploration to 1850.* Indianapolis, Ind.: W. K. Stewart Company, 1915.

——, ed. *Messages and Letters of William Henry Harrison.* Indianapolis, Ind.: Indiana Historical Collections, VII, 1922.

Goebel, Dorothy Burns. *William Henry Harrison: A Political Biography.* Indianapolis, Ind.: Historical Bureau of the Indiana Library and Historical Department, 1926.

Greene, George E. *History of Old Vincennes and Knox County, Indiana.* Chicago: 1911.

History of Knox & Daviess Counties, Indiana. Chicago: Goodspeed Publishing Company, 1886.

Illinois Historical Collections.

Illinois State Historical Society Journal.

Indiana Historical Collections.

Indiana Magazine of History, The.

Jacobs, Wilbur R. *Wilderness Politics and Indian Gifts: The Northern Colonial Frontier, 1748–1763.* Stanford, Calif.: Stanford University Press, 1950.

Kellogg, Louise Phelps. *The British Regime in Wisconsin and the Northwest.* Madison, Wis.: State Historical Society of Wisconsin, 1935.

——. *The French Regime in Wisconsin and the Northwest.* Madison, Wis.: State Historical Society of Wisconsin, 1925.

Law, Judge J. H. *The Colonial History of Vincennes.* Vincennes, Ind.: 1858.

Linley, Harlow, ed. *Indiana as Seen by Early Travelers: A Collection of Reprints from Books of Travel, Letters and Diaries Prior to 1830.* Indianapolis, Ind.: Indiana Historical Commission, 1916.

McDermott, John Francis, ed. *The French in the Mississippi Valley.* Urbana, Ill.: University of Illinois Press, 1965.

Parkman, Francis. *France and England in North America* (9 vols.). New York: Frederick Ungar Publishing Company, 1965. (Reprinted from the text of 1865.)

Phillips, Paul C. "Vincennes in Its Relation to French Colonial Policy." *Indiana Magazine of History,* Vol. XVII.

Pittman, Philip. *Present State of the European Settlements on the Mississippi.* London: 1770.

Powell, Lyman P. *Historic Towns of the Western States.* New York: Putnam, 1901.

Quaife, Milo M., ed. "Fort Knox Orderly Book, 1793–1797." *Indiana Magazine of History,* Vol. XXXII.

Roy, Pierre-Georges. *Sieur de Vincennes Identified.* Indianapolis, Ind.: C. E. Pauley & Company, n. d. (Indiana Historical Society Publications, Vol. VII, No. 1.)

Smith, H. M. *Historical Sketches of Old Vincennes.* Vincennes: 1902.

Somes, Joseph Henry VanderBurgh. *Old Vincennes.* New York: Graphic Books, 1962.

Thomas, David. *Travels Through the Western Country in the Summer of 1816.* Auburn, N.Y.: 1819.

Thornbrough, Gayle, ed. *Outpost on the Wabash, 1787–1791.* Indianapolis, Ind.: Indiana Historical Society, 1957.

Tucker, Glenn. *Tecumseh: Vision of Glory.* Indianapolis, Ind.: The Bobbs-Merrill Company, Inc., 1956.

Volney, Constantine F. *A View of the Soil and Climate of the United States of North America.* Philadelphia: 1804.

Watts, Florence Goold. "Fort Knox: Frontier Outpost on the Wabash, 1787–1816," *Indiana Magazine of History,* Vol. 62 (March 1966).

———. "Some Vincennes Documents of 1772," *Indiana Magazine of History,* Vol. 34.

Webster, Homer J. *William Henry Harrison's Administration of Indiana Territory.* Indianapolis, Ind.: Sentinel Printing Company, 1907.

Withers, Alexander Scott. *Chronicles of Border Warfare.* Cincinnati: The R. Clarke Company, 1895.

Index

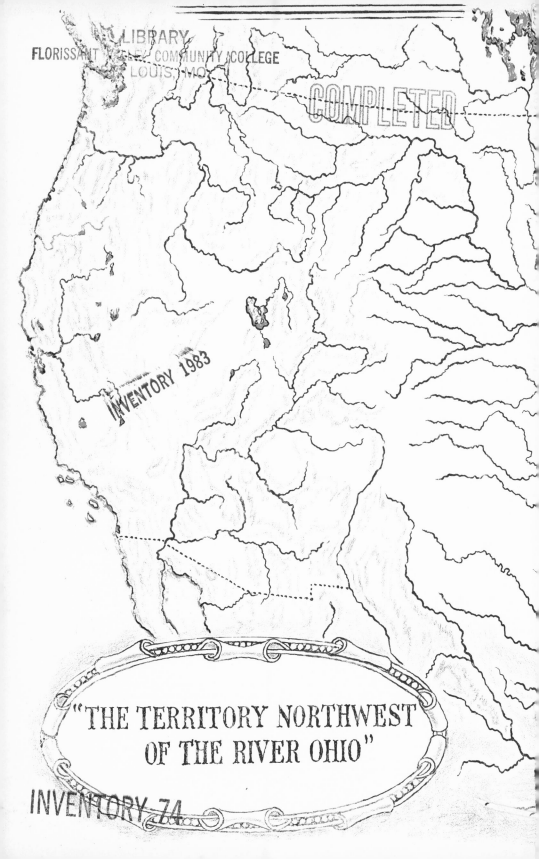

LIBRARY
FLORISSANT VALLEY COMMUNITY COLLEGE
ST. LOUIS, MO.

COMPLETED

INVENTORY 1983

"THE TERRITORY NORTHWEST
OF THE RIVER OHIO"

INVENTORY 74

Typography and Binding Design
by
CARL A. KOENIG

ABOUT THE AUTHOR

August Derleth is considered one of the last of the great authors writing about the American Middle West. Over thirty years ago he began carving out his own special Midwestern literary area and is one of the most prolific American writers (more than 100 books, plus countless articles and poems in magazines and newspapers). His two monumental novel cycles—*The Sac Prairie Saga* and *The Wisconsin Saga*—are so widely esteemed that alone they would justify Sinclair Lewis' designation of Mr. Derleth in 1939 as "a writer of the first importance."

Mr. Derleth is a leading authority on Henry David Thoreau and Sherlock Holmes. (He is a charter member of the Baker Street Irregulars in this country.) Aside from his busy writing schedule, Mr. Derleth is also the founder and director of Arkham House: Publishers, and literary editor of *The Capital Times* of Madison, Wisconsin. He owns the world's largest collection of comics, as well as a fine stamp collection. In his leisure time he enjoys chess, swimming, and walks through the countryside of his beloved Wisconsin.